Knowing
the Context

Elements of Preaching
O. Wesley Allen Jr., series editor

Knowing the Context

Frames, Tools, and Signs for Preaching

James R. Nieman

Fortress Press
Minneapolis

To JoAnn
. . . daß meine Freude in euch bleibe
und eure Freude völlig werde

KNOWING THE CONTEXT
Frames, Tools, and Signs for Preaching

Cover image: © iStockphoto.com/Igor Skrynnikov
Cover and book design: John Goodman

Library of Congress Cataloging-in-Publication Data
Nieman, James R., 1956–
  Knowing the context : frames, tools, and signs for preaching / James R. Nieman.
    p. cm. — (Elements of preaching)
  Includes bibliographical references and index.
  ISBN 978-0-8006-6262-2 (alk. paper)
  1. Preaching. I. Title.
  BV4211.3.N54 2008
  251—dc22
                                2008011154

The paper used in this publication meets the minimum requirements of American National Standard for Information Sciences—Permanence of Paper for Printed Library Materials, ANSI Z329.48-1984.

Manufactured in the U.S.A.

Contents

Editor's Foreword

Preparing beginning preachers to stand before the body of Christ and proclaim the word of God faithfully, authentically, and effectively Sunday after Sunday is and always has been a daunting responsibility. As North American pastors face pews filled with citizens of a postmodern, post-Christendom culture, this teaching task becomes even more complex. The theological, exegetical, and homiletical skills that preachers need for the future are as much in flux today as they have ever been in Western Christianity. Thus providing seminary students with a solid but flexible homiletical foundation at the start of their careers is a necessity.

Traditionally, professors of preaching choose a primary introductory textbook that presents a theology of proclamation and a process of sermon development and delivery from a single point of view. To maintain such a singular point of view is the sign of good writing, but it does at times cause problems for learning in pluralistic settings. One approach to preaching does not fit all. Yet a course simply surveying all of the homiletical possibilities available will not provide a foundation on which to build either.

Furthermore, while there are numerous introductory preaching textbooks from which to choose, most are written from the perspective of Euro-American males. Classes supplement this view with smaller homiletical texts written by women and persons of color. But a pedagogical hierarchy is nevertheless set up: the white male voice provides the main course and women and persons of color provide the side dishes.

Elements of Preaching is a series designed to help professors and students of preaching—including established preachers who want to develop their skills in specific areas—construct a sound homiletical foundation in a conversational manner. This conversation is meant to occur at two levels. First, the series as a whole deals with basic components found in most introductory preaching classes: theology of proclamation, homiletical contexts, biblical interpretation, sermonic claim, language and imagery, rhetorical form, delivery, and worship. But each element is presented by a different scholar, all of whom represent diversity in terms of gender, theological traditions (Baptist, Disciple of Christ, Lutheran, Presbyterian, and United Methodist), and ethnicity (African American, Asian American, and Euro-American). Instead of bringing in different voices at the margin of the preaching class, Elements of Preaching creates a conversation around the central topics of an introductory course without foregoing essential instruction concerning sermon construction and embodiment. Indeed, this level of conversation is extended beyond the printed volumes through the Web site www.ElementsofPreaching.com.

Second, the individual volumes are written in an open-ended manner. The individual author's particular views are offered but in a way that invites, indeed demands, the readers to move beyond them in developing their own approaches to the preaching task. The volumes offer theoretical and practical insights, but at the last page it is clear that more must be said. Professors and students have a solid place to begin, but there is flexibility within the class (and after the class in ministry) to move beyond these volumes by building on the insights and advice they offer.

In this volume, James R. Nieman introduces readers to the challenge of contextual preaching. Anyone who has ever tried to repreach a sermon that was really effective in one setting only to find it falling flat in another knows the importance of preparing each sermon for a specific context. While the good news of Jesus Christ may have eternal relevance, sermonic expressions of the gospel do not. We do not simply offer the gospel when we preach, we offer it to a particular community who has particular needs and concerns as they gather in a particular time and place. Nieman offers pastors tools for discovering, analyzing, and addressing issues that exist in and affect a particular congregation as it strives to live out its identity as the body of Christ and its members strive to be faithful Christians in particular circumstances. Often when preachers consider context, they are thinking primarily of the immediate circumstances of the week—political events, pastoral crises, administrative challenges. Nieman, however, takes us deeper into the dynamics of congregational existence. The kinds of contextual concerns to which he introduces us cannot be fixed with a single twenty-minute sermon. Instead, they must be addressed in a range of pastoral approaches and considered as one prepares sermons week after week, year after year. Preachers who adopt Nieman's methodology in dealing with the contextual element of proclamation will find their preaching ministry reaching levels of relevance that effect real change in their congregations.

O. Wesley Allen Jr.

Introduction

Paying attention to context is often trumpeted as a virtue. Effective and life-long pastoral ministry demands it, we are told, not least of all the specific ministry of preaching. This book supports that view while questioning its apparent simplicity. Contextual awareness ought not be reduced to a slogan in theological education and ministerial practice, a byword affirmed by all that therefore needs no further thought. It is one thing to claim a preacher must know the context but quite another to ask why this is so, how it might happen, and what should be done with the results. This book invites you into these deeper and more difficult dimensions of the subject, to adopt a workable discipline and its transformative consequences.

This book is a teaching text, which is not the same as saying it exists solely for classroom or coursework. It stands within a series of brief volumes, each of which introduces a specific aspect fundamental to preaching. As such, it is partly intended for the beginning preacher enrolled in seminary or participating in other forms of basic theological education for ministry. In such cases this text will doubtless be used alongside others under an instructor's guidance to supplement lectures or reinforce experiential learning. While this is one of its purposes, there are others that may be just as valuable. As a teaching text, this book is also for the experienced preacher whose classroom days are now a hazy memory but for whom continued growth in ministry remains a vibrant concern. It aims at accessibility for the self-motivated pastor/scholar who simply wishes to be introduced to a topic that was overlooked years ago or only handled in a cursory and undeveloped way. As a teaching text, therefore, this book offers you a learning partnership in discovering the ways context and preaching can relate, whether you are a novice, an adept, or somewhere in between.

You can better accept that offer by knowing where our mutual journey is headed. The structure of this book involves three simple moves, starting from rationale, moving to strategies, and concluding with challenges. The *rationale* is developed in chapter 1 ("How Context Matters in Preaching"). Strange as it sounds, there is little clarity or agreement on this neglected matter. It is crucial, however, that we grapple with how context is built into the preaching task and how preaching can have any impact at all upon a specific context. Special attention is given to the nature of preaching as an occasional, situational, social, and cultural practice, and how our distinctive circumstances as preachers moti-vate our direct interest in context.

The *strategies* are developed in the ensuing three chapters. In chapter 2 ("Frames for Approaching Contexts"), you will learn preparatory steps to make your contextual study more efficient and effective. Doing so requires you to state a research problem, that is, the reason you as a preacher are interested in your specific context, and then frame that research in order to focus your study better. In chapter 3 ("Tools for Exploring Contexts"), you will learn con-textual study methods that provide a disciplined way to examine your setting carefully and responsibly. Four tools from qualitative field research are intro-duced, each strikingly similar to familiar pastoral skills but also with particular procedures and benefits. In chapter 4 ("Signs for Interpreting Contexts"), you will learn how to take the insights from contextual study and connect them to what you say in the pulpit. This calls for seeing the context as a set of theologi-cal signs that implicitly bear deeper claims, meanings, values, and worldviews with which preachers must engage. Each of these three chapters concludes by tracing a single case study through these various steps in order to show the strategies in use.

The *challenges* are developed in chapter 5 ("How Preaching Works with Context"). By returning to the case study from the previous chapters, we can see how preaching in that situation built upon contextual insights. We explore how preaching in that congregation related to other forms of ministry that were also affected by the contextual study. A careful commentary of an example sermon then follows, not as an ideal to be mimicked but a sample of how one preacher put contextual insights into homiletical action. Selections from other sermons in the same setting are also woven into that commentary. The chapter concludes with several broad guidelines that can contribute to durable practices for sound contextual preaching.

Acknowledgments

One of the delights of writing a book is the chance to thank those who con-tributed to its production. Wes Allen, who cooked up this series in his imagina-tion only to be saddled with becoming its general editor, has been an intrepid and irreverent colleague through the low points of professional meetings and the high points of caring about our discipline, and I am grateful for his invita-tion to write this volume. David Lott of Fortress Press has been a persistent and stalwart advocate for this long-needed series, and I am grateful that his efforts have led to a new set of resources available for many kinds of learn-ers. Many other people at Fortress, hidden and unknown to me, have handled and examined and fussed over this text, and I am indebted to their patient and professional care.

The greatest delight of writing this book, however, is the chance to dedicate it now to my pastor, who is also the most consistently engaging preacher I know. It always saddens me to learn when quite faithful people dread what they hear from the pulpit each week, which evidently amounts to vapid or ponderous religious speeches that say little of consequence and are offered with even less care. Such is not my plight. Every Sunday I can count upon the Scripture spread out as a feast, the good news of Christ soundly declared, and all of this related wisely and deeply to our rather messy congregation in its quite ordinary circumstances. Seemingly without effort but never without purpose, my pastor consistently opens the way for mercy and hope to resound in our context. I am thankful that for so many years she has been the preacher I get to hear and especially that for even longer we have been married. This book is in thanksgiving for JoAnn Post and in celebration of her nearly quarter-century of pastoral ministry.

Hartford Seminary
Winter 2007–2008

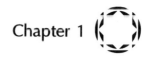

Chapter 1

How Context Matters in Preaching

No preacher strives to be irrelevant. It just gradually creeps into the pulpit, unbidden and unannounced. Surely its appearance reflects no lack of preparation. The Scripture was patiently studied, the sermon carefully composed, and the delivery thoroughly practiced. Even so, without warning, it slips into your preaching one Sunday morning. Though the sermon seemed off to a strong start, you now begin to notice glazed eyes, hear fidgeting and rustling, and palpably sense that no one is really listening. Why did this happen, and why now? Musing over this later, you can remember other sermons that were quite different, times when the room felt alive and the air electric and the whole assembly unshakably connected to what you were saying. Now, however, that bond seems broken and your confidence bruised.

To be irrelevant and find our preaching discounted sounds like a fate to avoid at all costs. Preachers often do so by treating it like a mechanical problem, something repaired by using the proper tools. A new device or technique, adeptly learned and consistently applied, will restore both the sermon's connection and the preacher's credibility.[1] Freshness is the key, the latest ideas, practices, or styles that pave the way to pulpit relevance. This approach is not accidental. It is the way of consumer marketing, packaging a product to be seen, selected, and sold. With preaching, however, it is a costly strategy. It buys into the craving for novelty in a society driven by desire and the decay that keeps desire alive. Whatever appeal it garners for the sermon is short lived, giving way to a hunger for the next new thing. The relevance that technical solutions offer is thin indeed and, ultimately, self defeating.

Such strategies betray a troubling lack of confidence about what preachers really do. Preaching is nothing less than declaring God's ways for us, the undeserved mercy that we know in Jesus and receive through the Spirit as a gift.[2] If this is the heart of preaching, can there be anything more relevant? Can we dress this up to be more potent or profound than it already is? Maybe the real problem is simply a lack of nerve on the part of the preacher. Instead of striving to reach to our listeners, perhaps we should proclaim scriptural basics unadorned by further efforts to make them more appealing. Just let the Word have its say.[3] Yet a nagging doubt arises here as well. Aware of our listeners' meager biblical knowledge, we have a pastoral concern for those who truly want to hear of *God's ways* but remain baffled about how these words can also be *for us*. The duty to make this connection in preaching cannot be piously sidestepped.

To repeat: No preacher strives to be irrelevant. If its unwelcome appearance cannot be dispelled, however, by more study, new techniques, or resolute will power, what can be done? That is the focus of this book. At a basic level, *contextual study* can be a crucial way toward more relevant and engaged preaching. As soon as this is said, though, a warning is needed. To explore our context (a term we examine in greater detail in the next chapter) should not become a preaching gimmick, another new tool for fixing a problem. This treats context superficially as a field of reception into which sermons are launched. Worse still, it treats those who hear sermons as hapless victims we manipulate by condescending to learn about them. Preaching is more than religious communication and its listeners are more than spiritual consumers.

Preaching is not really about bridging from an ancient and arcane scriptural world into a current and complex social reality, so that knowing more about each end of that bridge produces more effective communication. This functional view works just as easily with any historic text and its value for any later audience. Instead, preaching bears a living encounter between the God we know chiefly through Jesus and a contemporary people that trusts this God as the source of their life. This encounter happens not as a mental idea or a vague force but through direct divine participation in actual human reality. God risked identifying with Israel, both its glories and its shame. Jesus touched diseased bodies, accepting their wounds as his own. The Spirit visited fearful disciples, driving them beyond closed doors. Preaching represents just this kind of encounter with all who will listen, an embodied way God enters into our lives.

Context matters in preaching, therefore, for these theological reasons. The sermon announces how God meets us in the messiness and complexity of our lives. That is, preaching offers a contextual word, one that takes our particular setting seriously as the place where saving hope is concretely known. We need not escape our everyday reality in order to receive such a promise but instead learn the remarkable news that God bends to us through Jesus in the ordinariness of our existence. This is why preaching pays attention to context, in order to acclaim more richly and radically the abundant life with Jesus that can be ours here and now. We preach contextually, then, not merely because our preaching becomes more relevant but also so it more amply embodies a genuine encounter with Jesus.

Were theological grounds not enough, there is another reason that context matters for preaching. It has to do with the use, or really misuse, of language, an issue made vivid through two different lives. Picture a prison cell. The year is 1961, barely fifteen years after the end of the Second World War and right in the middle of the Cold War. The cell is in Jerusalem and its occupant is Adolf Eichmann, former propaganda minister for the Nazi regime in Germany, abducted in Buenos Aires by Israeli agents after having escaped trial years earlier. Jewish philosopher Hannah Arendt receives rare access to Eichmann during his trial on war crimes and tries to fathom the kind of man she has met. After hours of interviewing, she concludes that he displays "the banality of evil," referring neither to stupidity nor malice but to his shallow and boring character. At the heart of her analysis of Eichmann's deeds, responsible for heinous harm to millions, she notices something strange in the way he speaks:

> Eichmann, despite his rather bad memory, repeated word for word the same stock phrases and self-invented clichés . . . each time he referred to an incident or event of importance to him. Whether writing his memoirs in Argentina or in Jerusalem, whether speaking to the police examiner or to the court, what he said was always the same, expressed in the same words. The longer one listened to him, the more obvious it became that his inability to speak was closely connected with an inability to *think*, namely, to think from the standpoint of somebody else. No communication was possible with him, not because he lied but because he was surrounded by the most reliable of all safeguards against the words and the presence of others, and hence against reality as such.[4]

Picture now another prison cell. This one is not set long after the war but in its final days. The cell is in Berlin and its occupant is Dietrich Bonhoeffer, a Lutheran pastor suspected in a plot to kill Adolf Hitler, arrested by the very regime Eichmann's words legitimated. Many Christians today know Bonhoeffer through his earlier writings, stirring reflections on true discipleship and searing rejections of cheap grace. Perhaps his most important work, however, was penned in this prison cell during the months before his execution. These are his ethical essays, and much of their focus is on words. Bonhoeffer is concerned about what we say: phrases that after a time begin to sound true, but neither truly engage reality nor adopt the viewpoint of another person. His deepest social critique concerns language—not merely the overwhelming quantity of words—but especially their insubstantial quality that obscures honest thought and produces lies that enable suffering:

> Every word lives and has its home within a certain radius. . . . Every word should have and retain its own place. As a result of the increasing profligacy of public discourse in newspapers and the radio, the nature and limits of different words are no longer clearly perceived; in fact, what is distinctive about a personal word, for example, is nearly destroyed. Chatter has replaced authentic words. Words no longer have any weight. There is too much talking. Yet when the limits of different words blur together, when words become rootless, homeless, then what is said loses hold of the truth; indeed, at that point lying almost inevitably emerges. When the various orders of life no longer respect one another, then words become untrue.[5]

Although these reflections on misused language stretch back over half of a century, they still sound remarkably current. When massive job layoffs are called "right-sizing," government-authorized kidnapping is called "special rendition," and civilian deaths during wartime are called "collateral damage," then reality has been relabeled to obstruct a clear view of things as they are. When the airwaves and blogs become personal platforms for strident, callous opinions that are never held to account, humane discussion is muted and displaced by surplus verbiage. How can anyone take context seriously when awash not simply in many words, or many empty words, but words disconnected from reality? How can anyone take words seriously (including the ones we preach) if their preponderant use is to inflict real damage while masking what they inflict? We have already seen that context matters to preaching because God's Word embraces our ordinary lives—a theological concern. We now see another reason context matters to preaching, because the world's words evoke fixation on ourselves, detachment from others, and shallowness about our common plight—an equally theological concern. Preaching respects and explores context not only to declare more fully the living word God offers but also to confront more plainly the hollow words proffered in substitute.[6]

How Preaching Relates to Context

If context matters to preaching for serious theological reasons, we must still examine the challenge from the opposite direction. Extensive contextual study is pointless for the ministry of proclamation if preaching cannot do anything with or about context. At one level, this involves the outcomes of preaching, which remain truly mysterious. We cannot know beforehand the concrete results a sermon will have on a congregation or context, and even afterward the effect may be indirect and sketchy. Preachers soon learn that the sermon's consequences arise by the Spirit's unpredictable movement through the word declared, a matter of faith and not sight. Rather than looking at the outcomes of the sermon, however, we can consider preaching in another way: as a practice. Practices are simply tangible actions that are socially embedded, meaningful for users, offering strategies for right use while seeking an intended purpose. Baseball pitching, piano playing, and cooking are all practices, as are (closer to our purposes) hymn singing, public praying, and preaching.[7] Understood in this way, there actually are a few typical features that make preaching surprisingly adept at engaging contextual realities.

First, preaching is *occasional*. Obviously, preaching is not a constant or continuous activity like our heartbeat or breathing, so immersed in every moment as to be inseparable. Nor, however, is it detached from the rhythms of our days and lives, floating motionless beyond time in an eternal realm. Instead, preaching happens "occasionally," at times set aside for its specific use, especially in the event of worship. Sometimes these occasions follow an orderly pattern, such as the weekly assembly on Sunday or the annual cycle of the church festivals and seasons. Just as often, though, preaching comes about in irregular yet still profoundly eventful moments, such as gatherings connected with marriage, death, healing, or crisis. The point is that a sermon happens both *at a time* (on occasions) and *due to time* (for occasions). Whether planned in advance or apparently spontaneous, preaching is not self-generated. It is called for, and for a reason: to address the times in which it occurs.

Therefore, preaching can attend to context because it is a *timely* word. Paradoxically, although preachers utter something treasured as worthwhile for all generations, they can only do so within their own generation. This is actually a liberating realization, for we need not "say it all" in a timelessly true yet assuredly remote sermon, but simply the word that is enough for today. It also imposes an obligation on every sermon to be attuned to what is happening now, since speaking to anything else would literally be a waste of time. Fortunately, preaching has the advantage of unfolding not only *in* time but also *through* it. The time of the sermon can be used to evoke a new reality for listeners to enter, one that might be drawn from Scripture, or visible in the lives of other faithful people, or aimed toward deeper memories and hopes. For this reason, preaching is no victim of its moment but creates new occasions, times of decisive encounter (*kairos*) or horizons of divine meaning (*eschaton*) that can reshape our lives even now. Precisely by paying attention to times and seasons, preaching therefore engages the context in order to challenge its assumed normalcy and envision life-giving alternatives.

Second, preaching is *situational*. Despite our ambitions, any sermon operates with only a limited direct reach. This is because its "placement" seeps through in language and structure, enabling us easily to perceive its intended hearers. No wonder preachers soon learn how deadly it is to repeat a sermon meant for others elsewhere, regardless how noble or trendy the source. Even the seemingly wide appeal of mass media sermons shows merely the range of broadcast technology, which still relies upon reproducing what is preached in a specific location before a particular audience. The point is basic and easily overlooked: sermons are inextricably embedded in situations, real settings with distinctive features. Moreover, sermons are thoroughly associated with bodies, being oral activities interiorized aurally. In their primary and direct settings, sermons are uttered by speakers in proximity to hearers who incorporate those words in relation to familiar surroundings. That is, preaching materially "takes place" both amidst physical spaces and within physical bodies. For whatever limits this creates, in the long run it is an asset. Defined by its particular place, preaching is distinctly able to pay attention to that place closely and realistically, patiently and amply engaging a setting through what is declared.

Therefore, preaching can attend to context because it is a *grounded* word. This is not how we usually think. We have somehow come to believe that the more universally or generically we speak, the more widely we will reach, when in fact such talk actually stands apart from lived reality and therefore appeals only superficially. By contrast, grounded preaching narrates something particular and concrete. When hearers meet this on their own terms in the specificity of their own lives, such preaching has greater impact than generalizations ever will. Beyond this matter of wide appeal, grounded preaching bears specific resources to affirm and to challenge a particular setting in powerful ways. On the one hand, it narrates the *mythic* dimension of a setting, respecting the assured worldviews, beliefs, and values ordinarily found there. On the other hand, it narrates a *parabolic* dimension of that same setting, interrupting what is acceptable in order to probe its credibility and faithfulness.[8] These two dimensions are involved whenever we ask, "Will it preach?" That familiar question bluntly challenges our intended words to withstand the situated scrutiny of a context's mythic and parabolic angles. Grounded preaching is always found someplace in particular where it must tell the whole truth, both what we like to hear and what we prefer to suppress. It therefore engages the context by narrating the breadth of the local story: its approved version, its contrary tales, and its emerging voices of hope.

Third, preaching is *social*. Although sermons occur at particular times in specific places, they are intended for real people. These people are not reducible to analytical concepts like social structure or organization. Nor are they best treated as independent individuals, separable integers who just happen to be together. Instead, preaching typically is a social event in a gathering that knows and sustains a group identity. It is an address from people to people that, among other things, speaks to what it means to be human as a participant in that group. Socially embedded and enacted, preaching engages what it means to be fully human in the company of others. That company of others is a special one for preaching, since it is called and assembled by God's word of life. That is, preaching typically happens in some form of church for the sake of its distinctive identity and mission. In this special group setting, preaching therefore speaks to what it means to be human beyond just what may be ethical (human agency and responsibility) or existential (human concerns and aspirations), all the way to what is faithful (true humanity as holy people created in and living toward the image of God).

Therefore, preaching can attend to context because it is a *personal* word. It personally encounters us with who we are and who we might yet be. At a basic level, we each bear a distinct personal identity that always stands in relation to other persons. Preaching first meets us at this empirical level of existence by unmasking the identities we receive from various groups, such as ethnicity, class, or beliefs. Sermons can name our enmeshment in these networks and systems that both grant a sense of belonging but also create constraints and impose biases. Sermons can also highlight the worldviews and interests that accompany such belonging, forcing us to ask whether these are appropriate forms of personhood (matters to which we will return in the next chapter). At a deeper level, we face a common human plight, sharing sorrows and hopes familiar to other persons. Preaching then meets us at this spiritual level of existence by inviting us to see our human dignity as a gift conferred by God's mercy. Sermons can clarify who we are through Christ for others, as persons in solidarity with other persons that they might know true life. Sermons can also impel us toward what is "seriously imaginable" as faithful people who bear the gospel in a given time and place.[9] Personal preaching addresses this entire empirical and spiritual range of being human. It therefore engages the context by pointing to what is needed there for genuine human thriving.

Fourth, preaching is *cultural*. We have just observed that preaching happens personally through human groups. The broader work of such groups is culture, the ways people mark off who they are and give shape to the spaces they inhabit. Culture takes whatever is naturally given and redirects it for the purpose of making sense of the world.[10] As a result, this kind of cultural work can often have a sweeping impact. For example, one basic form of culture happens when physical bodies and ordinary sound become the raw materials of language, enabling human communication. By employing widely available forms like conversation, stories, and sayings, language helps people to bond together, interpret a common setting, express shared values, and plan for their mutual efforts. The work of language is therefore just one potent example of how culture allows us to name and claim a greater sense of what human life can or should be. It is exactly this cultural currency in which preaching trades. It is embedded in the cultural activity of language (not to mention other forms of culture as well). As such, preaching can therefore enter into significant contact with such crucial cultural enterprises as communal affiliation, societal understanding, normative assertions, and ultimate purposes.

Therefore, preaching can attend to context because it is a *symbolic* word. Since culture is something we impose upon nature, it is always at heart a symbolizing activity. Although symbols are often considered insubstantial and weak, they in fact represent a powerful way cultural forms operate, through which we express our allegiances, failures, disagreements, and hopes. Preaching is ultimately able to do something in a context by working through cultural forms, chiefly, but not strictly, that of language, to engage this symbolic significance (a topic to which we will return at length in chapter 4). By deploying the local language at hand, preaching meets a context literally on its own cultural terms. It can analyze those terms to reveal their underlying anxieties and biases, the symbolic freight of the local setting. It can draw from those same terms as from a symbolic storehouse, calling forth language that appeals deeply to its hearers. Yet preaching is neither innocent bystander nor hapless neophyte in this process. Instead, it goes further to interact with those terms by drawing upon still others, the biblical and theological symbols available from the wealth of Christian tradition. In these ways, preaching can even challenge and propose an alternate symbolic vision for what is life giving and bears God's aims for humankind. By being attuned to the symbolic, preaching therefore engages the context through words that work deeply and in ways few other cultural expressions can.

This section began by asking what it is about the practice of preaching that lets it connect with and affect a given context. The answer is that preaching happens *sometime* (it is occasional and thus a timely word) and *somewhere* (it is situational and thus a grounded word), involving *somebody* (it is social and thus a personal word) and occurring *somehow* (it is cultural and thus a symbolic word). Our detailed exploration of these four features was no intellectual exercise, though, for how the question is answered affects how to study context for the sake of preaching (which is the focus of the next three chapters). One of the daunting aspects of any contextual study is the overwhelming amount of information that can be gathered about a particular setting. Vast amounts of interesting material can be collected that, in reality, make scant difference in how to preach more effectively, or involve matters better addressed through activities other than preaching. By contrast, the features presented in this section suggest how to focus contextual research that is especially attuned to the practice of preaching. From the very start, therefore, we must be clear that our interest in investigating a context should be driven by the extent to which such study helps our preaching become more timely, grounded, personal, and symbolic. Amply and accurately understood, the practice of preaching refines both what is worth considering in a context and what is not.

Historical Views of Contextual Preaching

The turn to contextual studies in recent scholarship has rightly been criticized for its occasional tendency to foreground the present situation at the expense of any historical depth. The same criticism could be made of our attention here to preaching and context. We need the humility to remember that we are not the first generation ever to have considered the importance of context for preaching or how preaching shapes context. Indeed, if the practice of preaching includes at least the features named above (recognizing, of course, that there are other features besides these), then virtually any sermon esteemed as effective in its own day would necessarily have been contextually attuned. Yet there is also little point in demonstrating across the span of church history that good preaching has been good in part because it engaged its setting. To be sure, a fascinating story could be told about what specifically contributed in various periods of history to those cases when preaching was most timely, grounded, personal, and symbolic—that is, deeply contextual. That longer tale diverts from our central purposes here, however.

We are better served to ask about those forebears for whom context became an explicit consideration in their view of preaching. The focus is then more narrowly on those whose overt attention to setting was integral to how they thought Christian proclamation should work, rather than on preachers whose contextual sensitivity is evident only implicitly or who reflected little on the practice itself. While the historical material here is smaller, it is still too massive for our present aims. What we can profitably do, however, is foreground a few revealing instances, not as comprehensive of an entire history but as demonstrative of diverse reasons for attending to context in relation to preaching. On the one hand, this reassures us that we are neither alone nor novel in these efforts but part of a long and venerable tradition from which there is still much to learn. On the other hand, this highlights distinctive motivations for studying context, both those of enduring importance and those of special significance for us today.

Arguably the earliest extended treatment of how to preach was Augustine's *On Christian Doctrine*. The first three-quarters of that work, written near the end of the fourth century, address preparation for preaching, mainly in terms of interpreting biblical texts. Augustine completed his text roughly twenty-five years later with a fourth part that focused on the act of preaching itself. It was this section that showed his interest in context, and for reasons that pertain to his own background. Like nearly all Christian preachers before him, Augustine had extensive training in classical Ciceronian rhetoric. He drew upon those categories and strategies in describing how to preach. For example, he affirmed that preaching involved not only a publicly argued word (*logos*) presented through a speaker's character (*ethos*) but also the reception of that word through the hearers' emotions (*pathos*). Attention to the actual human gathering also mattered because the aims of the sermon were to teach, delight, and move its hearers toward Christian faithfulness.[11] Even preaching language must be fitting for those who have assembled in order to accommodate the mysteries of God to the widest range of people. Contrary to accepted practice, Augustine thought sermons should vary the styles known as *grand* (ornate eloquence), *subdued* (ordinary expression), and *moderate* (measured and in-between) in ways appropriate to hearers. "When a speech carries on in a single style, it is less absorbing for the listener, but when there is transition from one style to another it has a smoother flow, even if it is rather long."[12] Strange as this approach and its conventions about speaking may sound to us now, Augustine simply held a concern we still share, to promote well-crafted sermons that make the treasures of the faith fully available for typical hearers. This was what drove his engagement with the preaching context. It is important to note that his motivation was *rhetoric*.

As a defense of his reluctance to be elevated to the papacy in the year 590, Gregory the Great wrote what eventually became the single most lasting and influential exposition of ministerial duties and burdens, *The Book of Pastoral Rule*. His concern was less about preaching than the role of priests and the character needed for such service. Even so, the third and by far longest portion of this work relates directly to our discussion. In it, Gregory described thirty-six contrasting pairs of human types that preachers regularly had to teach and admonish, such as the poor and the rich, the joyful and the sad, or the wise and the dull. Doubtless drawing from his own broad pastoral experience, Gregory astutely commented on these different kinds of people and what was needed to suit the words of instruction to the capacities of each. So far, this advice sounds very similar to that of Augustine but with an important difference. The larger purpose for understanding the lives of listeners in this detail was in order to prepare for confession, healing, and amendment of life. Although Gregory was also concerned about how to reach people effectively, he saw preaching's real aim as contributing to the cure of souls. "Hence, too, every teacher, in order to edify all in the one virtue of charity, must touch the hearts of hearers by using one and the same doctrine, but not by giving to all one and the same exhortation."[13] The situated need for different forms of care directed Gregory's engagement with the preaching context. His central motivation was therefore explicitly *pastoral*.

Recognizing the dreary state of preaching at the start of the twelfth century, Guibert of Nogent responded with a brutally honest analysis, *How to Make a Sermon*. Less a method for preaching than a plea for improvement, it marked the gradual shift toward later Franciscan and Dominican preaching reforms. At heart, Guibert was distressed about the isolation of preachers from the spiritual needs of their hearers. This left clerics reluctant if not unwilling to preach because preaching was in poor repute, listeners were not worth improving, and preachers were miserly with their knowledge. Yet not to preach was to steal divine gifts for private benefit. Guibert saw preaching as the public obligation to teach doctrinal truths by opening up Scripture. Most of his treatise therefore explained the medieval fourfold approach to biblical interpretation (the historical, allegorical, tropological, and anagogical senses of Scripture), emphasizing how this could profit many different sermon listeners. Learned preachers should both explore such scriptural richness and "consider the weak ability of those who silently listen and that it would be better for them to receive a few points with pleasure than a great many of which none will be retained . . . "[14] This engagement with the preaching context was driven by the desire to open up biblical insights to common believers. While there were obvious rhetorical and pastoral overtones, Guibert's motivation was a basic concern for *teaching*.

Drawing upon hundreds of years of preaching in African American congregations, Henry Mitchell has more recently reflected about yet another reason to pay attention to context. Starting with the dialogical form of such preaching, its characteristic call-and-response style, he carefully teased apart what that meant about the black context in particular. In terms of performance, this style conveys a close relationship between preacher and listeners. Both parties to the sermon know each other and thrive upon interplay and conversation in the preaching event. In terms of worldview, the style reflects familiar insights and perspectives. Preachers know the weight that key phrases or images carry for their listeners precisely because everyone has been affected by related cultural and ethnic forces. Encompassing these, however, is an experience of racism and its attendant harm. In this light, the dialogue style becomes a vehicle for telling the truth about society. Sermons take seriously the "felt need" of real people, their cries of pain and hopes for relief. "Black preaching at its best has remained focused on problems that people confront daily and feel real needs in meeting. . . . The Black preacher has had to give strength for the current day's journey, the guidance and vision for extended survival in an absurdly trying experience."[15] Black preachers, like those from other cultures facing hardship and abuse, engage the preaching context for the sake of deliverance. The motivation is nothing less than *justice*.

Spare as they are, these few cases illustrate quite different reasons for paying attention to the context. They may in turn cause us to recall other times in the history of Christian preaching when contextual considerations moved to the foreground. None of these earlier motivations is entirely alien to us, and they press us to ask what ours may be. Beyond this, our continuity with each instance may help us refine or even critique our reasons for studying any preaching context today. If we are driven by rhetoric, will our study grant access to divine mysteries, as Augustine intended? If by pastoral care, will our study lead to healing, as Gregory hoped? If motivated by teaching, will true wisdom result, as Guibert proposed? If by justice, will contextual insight produce liberating action, as black preaching has sought? Such scrutiny should also remind us that any reasons for examining context can be easily distorted by other aims, such as rhetorical manipulation, pastoral compliance, teacher dependency, or social contentment.

These antecedents also remind us that our experience of context differs from that of earlier preachers in important ways. Instead of being naturally led from preaching toward context, we today find contextual realities unavoidably forced upon our preaching. Context is not a passive landscape for preachers to contemplate as they wish, but an active and contested site that often sets the terms for whether or how sermons will be understood. There is a heightened urgency about context. For one thing, we live in profoundly unsettled times, even to the point of crisis.[16] Such extensive change means that basic contextual concerns are increasingly difficult for preachers to identify and address. Compounding this, global factors impinge upon every local setting as never before.[17] This enmeshment means that preachers find it harder to discern where or how their words should be actually directed. All told, the tumultuous and diffuse quality of contemporary situations makes it especially important that context receive direct and intentional focus in the practice of preaching.

Fortunately, several significant changes make this an opportune moment to study context in and for the church. Religious leaders have recovered an appreciation of the local assembly as a basic level of ecclesial existence.[18] As a result, there is a new desire to grasp the distinctiveness and diversity of those who faithfully gather in particular places. Theological scholars have also displayed growing respect for concrete settings that potently contribute to faith claims and practices.[19] Enacted beliefs are now treated with greater value in order to understand what is happening theologically at the local level. Finally, homiletics teachers have also made a noticeable turn toward the listener in their approach to preaching. Because actual hearers actively shape the meaning of the proclamatory event, this consequently affects the preparation and structure of sermons.[20] In these various ways, therefore, we stand amidst an increasingly open and eager interest in churches for sustained conversation about context, which has encouraged preachers in particular to take up this matter more directly.

The urgency of contextual forces today, combined with the ecclesial openness to explore these, certainly sets the stage for our distinctive interest in context. There is a remaining factor, however. Scholarly resources are newly at our disposal for studying context responsibly and thoroughly. These allow a more sophisticated grasp of ministry settings than was previously available. Earlier generations of preachers may have been highly motivated to understand their situations, but without an orderly, intentional, and direct form of research, they could rely only on general impressions. By contrast, we are now able to use disciplined methods for observation and interpretation in order to notice where and when we preach. These approaches often borrow from social and cultural research but with a special sensitivity to the ministry needs and proclamatory concerns of the contemporary church. Access to disciplined inquiry is therefore the most striking way we approach the preaching context differently than our ancestors. Such inquiry constitutes the very heart of this book and forms the substance of the next three chapters.

Chapter 2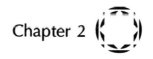

Frames for Approaching Contexts

Suppose you have clarified exactly why you need to understand better the context in which you preach. Suppose further that your motivations are the best imaginable. Perhaps you simply want people to hear God's mercy more concretely and encounter it more deeply. Maybe you even hope to show how Christ's abundant life for us implies a specific call to justice for all. Whatever the reason, you're ready to begin studying your situation . . . but how? The natural impulse is just to get out into the congregation and community in order to experience what is happening. While that urge shows commendable zeal, it also rapidly leads to exhaustion. Out of the many things around you, what must you really notice, which of these should you remember, and why? The risk in such a naïve plunge into context is becoming overwhelmed by too much information to absorb, let alone make useful in relation to preaching. A disciplined strategy is needed from the outset. That is the purpose of this chapter and the two that follow.

Virtually any approach to field research for contextual study follows a similar sequence. First comes collecting information about the situation in broad overview, then narrowing that material to what is most important to pursue for purposes of the study, and last analyzing what remains for patterns of meaning and significance.[1] The process seems simple and direct, fueling the eagerness to get started. What the sequence masks, however, is that such research does not actually begin with collecting but with earlier moves that require careful thinking and planning. Lest you despair that this is yet another way academic scholarship makes things harder and more complicated than they need to be, be advised that there is something serious at stake. Bluntly put, the failure to think ahead before studying a context risks mostly or entirely wasting your time. Such study is profoundly inefficient, unless you lack neither time nor resources and are thus indifferent about squandering both. At best, this kind of research will amass a "data dump," an immense amount of vaguely interesting information about your setting that is, even so, mostly unneeded. More likely, this approach will be a distraction from your primary research interest, which in this case involves how preaching can be more fully engaged with its context. Worst of all, what you learn may be gravely distorted and even impede your preaching with haphazard and untested insights whose value is scant if not illusory.

Scholars have learned to begin earlier and elsewhere. This book does not advocate that preachers need to become trained ethnographers in order to improve their sermons. Quite to the contrary, the next chapter will take pains to note how the most reliable tools for learning about context have fascinating links to several basic pastoral skills and roles. Even so, we can learn a few commonsense insights from formal fieldwork, even if these approaches are far more elaborate than we need. Three of these insights have already been implied. First, studying a context should happen for a reason, a motivation that the researcher has somewhere in mind. Second, studying a context involves a discipline, an orderly path instead of a chaotic melee. Third, studying a context calls for thinking ahead, planning in advance of any fieldwork. Combining these three, we can discern a basic yet frequently ignored principle: when you know what you seek, there is a better chance of finding it. Of course, this principle can be corrupted to justify bias (finding only what you want to see) or sloppiness (seeking so much that everything you find matters). Honestly employed, however, it provides focus and guidance. When your driving goal for contextual study is clearly named beforehand, you can sort out which insights will contribute directly to that goal and the steps needed to acquire those insights.

This is nothing other than learning to identify a research problem. Again, the point is not to bend pastoral ministry into some form of academic scholarship. Instead, a research problem at heart incorporates the features we expect of any question whose answer will make a difference to someone. It begins by naming a *topic*: what specific area you are trying to explore. It then poses a *question*: what you do not know within that topic but need to understand. It is not complete, however, unless it also states *significance*: what matters about answering this question, including likely benefits for finding an answer or costs for not doing so.[2] This all sounds terribly stilted and formal, until we recognize it as the common pattern of everything from mundane investigation (finding an affordable local plumber who can keep a leak from becoming a disaster) to lifetime pursuits (reading about the Civil War in order to gain perspective on contemporary issues). It also outlines how we prepare for preaching every week: "I am studying the fifth chapter of John [topic] to learn the background history to the pool of Bethzatha where Jesus once intervened [question], because it reminds me of a similar bondage from which we are freed [significance]." No preacher really says it this way, of course, but that just means the pattern is internalized. By elaborating the process, we can see that we already know how to study something for a purpose that makes a difference for others, a realistic goal to attain in a process that is not endless.

Unlike preaching, contextual study is not an already internalized process, so we need to be more explicit at the beginning to state something like a research problem. Fortunately, there are certain limits already in place. As far as we are concerned, for example, our focus is always some form of inquiry into what makes for more contextually engaged preaching. That is, we do not seek a descriptive overview of an unfamiliar setting or a taxonomy of special social relations there, as a cultural anthropologist might during years of field research. Our research problem ultimately pertains to preaching in relation to a particular context (a term explored in the next section of this chapter). In addition, we are not innocent about that task or setting but have honestly examined what is at stake for us and motivates our interest in context (as treated in the final section of the previous chapter). The point is that the context itself will not provide the topic, question, and significance for our study. We need instead to venture a solid pastoral hunch about the underlying issue, the contextual puzzle that, if better understood, would suggest concrete strategies for engagement through preaching. Whatever that puzzle is, the goal for addressing it cannot be merely utilitarian, such as effective communication or heightened sensitivity to local concerns. Though worthy, these goals are insufficient in light of the larger pastoral orientation of preaching. A contextual research problem for preachers should be ultimately and unashamedly theological in aim, such as seeking more compelling forms of witness to Christ amidst a particular gathering of the faithful.

Several years ago, a preacher I knew demonstrated how a clear research problem can become a natural part of pastoral life. It began with noticing something she couldn't explain. Although the typical and longtime members of her congregation were solidly middle class in terms of income, education, and work, a small but noticeable group of newcomers were starting to show up at worship. These persons endured what she called "labored lives." Few had any education beyond high school, employment was often piecemeal and poorly paid, and their households were complicated blends of divorce, partnership, and remarriage, rife with abuse and crisis. Yet there they were in church, sometimes sporadically but always attentive to her sermons. They counted her as their pastor, a claim made vivid through their urgent phone calls from the emergency room, police station, or funeral home. The question that baffled this pastor, however, was how she had ever connected with them. What did they hear from the pulpit that spoke to these lives so different from her own? Stating that question helped her acknowledge other places of ignorance, including how little she knew about the daily life of these parishioners, from their occasional despair to their larger delights and dreams. The result was a simple and manageable investigation conducted during two separate months of the same year, in which a small sampling of these people led her through their days, from home to work to play and back again. She wanted to know what mattered to them, how she was already speaking to this, and what she might be missing. It may not sound like much, but this was nothing other than a field study focused on one aspect of the context deemed to be particularly important for her preaching ministry. In fact, we could restate it as a formal research problem: "I am studying the daily lives of socially struggling members in the congregation [topic] to learn the values, patterns, and symbols significant to them [question], so I can more intentionally engage these through preaching the good news of forgiveness and hope [significance]."

We have advocated clarifying a research problem, formally or otherwise, so fieldwork will have focus and direction, enabling an efficient and workable contextual study that matters. Instead of absorbing everything at once, this lets you examine only what will be most revealing for now. Your study can also be improved by other forms of advance planning. For example, you can call on others from your ministry setting whenever possible to help you identify a significant contextual concern. This strategy, typical to participatory action research,[3] has the added benefits of revealing the ministry implications for a contextual issue far beyond preaching and involving people other than the preacher in what is learned. Another improvement is to refine the research problem by imposing a frame on it. Later in this chapter, we will examine three approaches to framing, which will in turn suggest the appropriate tools for actual contextual study. Before that, however, one other kind of advance planning is crucial. We must pause to consider the field of experience and raw materials we intend to study. Specifically, what is meant when we speak of context? More to the point, what concept of context best pertains to preaching?

Context Identified but Not Isolated

We have spoken rather casually about context, as if it were easy to specify what that term means. Theologian Max Stackhouse long ago challenged

whether matters were quite so clear by simply asking, "How big is a con
text? How long does it last? Who is in it and who is out of it, and how do
we know?"[4] No one can avoid these questions, whether the study is broadly
or (as in our case) narrowly defined. Yet even the most extensive fieldwork
restricts itself to describing a context that pertains only to its orienting
research problem. That is, a context is only as large as needed to address a
central question and lasts only until the fieldwork answers that question. This
approach may sound unsatisfying or arbitrary until we realize that "context"
is a concept artificially imposed upon complex situations for purposes of
inquiry, a mental convenience of sorts. Any effort to say what counts as a
relevant context is a construct, something devised in relation to why we are
looking at that context in the first place. Such a view is therefore not arbitrary but invested, examining a situation from a particular point of view. Nor
does this kind of investment necessarily produce a superficial or simplistic
understanding. Instead, those who clearly name their research interests are
better prepared to account for the breadth and depth that give a context its
distinctive character.

What particular investment do preachers therefore bring that helps to
identify the context more exactly? We noted in the previous chapter that
preaching is a timely word because it is occasional and a grounded word
because it is situational. This means preachers are interested in contexts
weighted more to the local than settings that are regional or global, and more
to the present than what happens significantly earlier or later.[5] Context is
not thereby isolated from the network of other relations in which it is always
embedded, however. The local context that most affects preaching still
remains within a larger ecology of institutional forces that generate opportunities and constraints. Likewise, the present context that most impinges
upon preaching is still influenced by the power of the traditions in which it
stands and the horizon toward which it tends. So embedded, the context
for preaching concerns mainly those relations and experiences with greatest
salience for those who are listening. They know who they are through direct
interaction with familiar people nearby and from that standpoint gain access
to the larger world. They know what matters in their history and hopes insofar as these contribute to the present and immediate future. In other words,
a preaching context is best identified by the active participants for whom it
makes a genuine difference. For related reasons, what counts as a relevant
context will differ from one congregation to the next, let alone among the
subgroups in any setting.

Once again, we are not promoting lengthy fieldwork but instead a compact exploration of context that can be useful for preaching. Even so, the

practices of larger field studies can also guide preachers toward what should and should not be considered as part of the context. One rule of thumb is that naming the research problem, discussed earlier in this chapter, is crucial for reining in the scope of the context and highlighting what to study therein. Preachers need not include everything as the defined context, as fascinating and consuming as that might be, but only what relates centrally to the specific preaching issue at hand. We acknowledge a biased point of view in this. Not every feature is equally interesting for us but mainly and mostly whatever is socially expressive and culturally freighted. This is true particularly because, as noted in the previous chapter, preaching is both a personal and a symbolic word.

Another rule of thumb is that the preaching context is centered in terms of its listeners. The worship gathering becomes a focal social setting for preaching through which broader contextual connections are recognized. We realize, of course, that preaching happens in ministries beyond formal worship, like institutional chaplaincy, and in multiple worship sites, like area-wide parishes. Amidst all this variety, the relevant preaching context is still recognized less by its boundaries than its relational core, those who actually listen. This does not mean, however, that we pay attention to them strictly in terms of when and where that listening occurs, such as Sunday morning in a church building. Contextual study goes on to explore the effective worlds that influence what people can hear and how they make sense of it. This includes what they experience at home, work, and wider social ambits, as well as through family, friends, and other significant contacts. These all contribute to the lived reality that listeners bring into the preaching moment, and for this reason are legitimate matters of contextual study.

A final rule of thumb is concerns the duration of our contextual study. Typical academic site research is driven by interests external to the context. For this reason, scholars study a context as long as they are granted access to it and until their central question is answered. Our approach is not similarly confined. You are trying to understand a context in which you, as a preacher, are already an insider, and the question before you is ongoing, just as your preaching extends from week to week and year to year. There is no predetermined close to your study, even though its intensity may wax or wane depending upon when you have opportunity to attend to the context carefully and intentionally. This persisting quality of the preaching context removes the pressure upon so many scholars not to miss a single detail. Study of a preaching context can instead be readily incorporated into the ordinary cycle of pastoral life, a pattern of exploration whose insights can grow alongside our preaching.

Different Ways to Frame Context

This chapter has so far treated topics seemingly far removed from preaching. The intent, however, has been to avert disaster when you look at the context for preaching. Learning about a context will not happen by chance or good intentions but requires thinking ahead about how you will deliberately study the situation. Yet this kind of study is surely not your full-time vocation, so it needs to be integrated into the ordinary course of pastoral life manageably, efficiently, and usefully. Toward this end, we have offered two general sorts of advice. First, you need to know and claim a research problem, identifying as clearly as possible your interest in the context. Since in this case that interest is for the sake of preaching, your exploration will already tend toward some aspects more than others, especially the social and cultural dimensions of the setting. Second, naming your research problem lets you identify the pertinent context. Much in your setting will not be directly relevant to this, so you consider only those events and materials that can truly inform your interests. Both sorts of advice are already forms of *framing*. That term will be used in several different ways in the rest of this chapter, but here the reference is to a frame as a design or plan, the conceptual map or invented strategy that allows a project to reach completion. In this sense, we speak of those who frame ideas or documents, like the framers of the U.S. Constitution. Knowing the research problem and limiting the contextual scope are both ways of framing (that is, designing) a study that can actually be achieved.

Three other kinds of framing are valuable for further refining the context you study because they all help with specifying the interests you bring to your research. Long ago, New Testament scholar Rudolf Bultmann posed the famous question, "Is presuppositionless exegesis possible?" He answered in the negative since the exegete "approaches the text with specific questions or with a specific way of raising questions and thus has a certain idea of the subject matter with which the text is concerned."[6] For similar reasons, we could say that there is no presuppositionless contextual study, a realization that is both honest and advantageous. Framing engages presuppositions by insisting that we declare our intentions. It forces us to be selective about which aspects of a context are useful in relation to our particular preaching concerns. The frames we detail here should not be misunderstood as fieldwork methods (which are the tools to be explored in the next chapter) but seen as filtering strategies that help us attune to specific dimensions of the context. In this way, they let us focus on one feature in a setting along with its predominant meanings, purposes, and values.[7]

At the start of your investigation, frames will be used before fieldwork begins in order to plan your study so that what you consider can be beneficially restricted. After that point, they will be iteratively deployed during the course of your work in a back-and-forth rhythm of framing, studying, and further reframing, as you clarify where you need to look once the fieldwork is already underway.[8] In what follows, each frame will be explained separately, along with typical contextual preaching challenges to which it is especially suited. At their best, frames offer distinctive ways to appreciate the context with fresh sensitivity and thus are quite helpful for keeping your research on track. Even so, they should be treated as working in concert rather than being utterly discrete, a matter to which we return at the close of this section.

Frame as Border

Perhaps the most typical way we imagine a frame is as an enclosure around something. This is how we speak of the frame for a portrait or window, or even a pair of eyeglasses. The visual and perceptual connotations are important for this use of the term. While often having its own appeal, this kind of frame serves mainly to direct our attention to whatever it contains, without obstruction or distraction. In reference to the study of context, such framing means to develop the bounded perspectives on a setting that can help us notice who people are. It gives us an orientation to the participants in a context, with special attention to cultural identity. Preachers therefore can find it useful for trying to understand how particular people in the congregation or its surroundings make sense of their lives and the worlds they occupy. If you are aware of a subgroup of listeners whose ways differ from your own or whose values you struggle to grasp, this kind of framing can help to focus your contextual study.

Cultural identity is probably the default way of framing a context, noting overt features and distinctions. In our day, this unfortunately has been further diminished to one kind only, the *ethnic frame*. Certainly ethnicity is important for showing the community commitments and mutual history that strongly shape people, as well as reinforcing customs, values, and behaviors. This frame reveals only one form of cultural identity, however, which in some contexts may not be the most important. We often overlook the *class frame* with its economic, labor, education, and status qualities. Attending to these can show a different slant on human worth, a person's place in the fabric of society, and views of personal authority. Also important is the use of the *belief frame* that highlights the religious claims and practices by which people are oriented to ultimate realities. Through this frame we can perceive stark differences among otherwise seemingly similar people, differences that affect life direction, decision making, and world interpretation.[9] Of course, many other frames of cultural identity might be more pertinent to your research problem, such as generation, region, gender, ableness, or sexual orientation. In any case, your framing should be open to several and not merely the most obvious or shopworn.

Preachers are understandably drawn to this kind of framing because it explains so much about the shared bonds among listeners. To frame in a regional or generational way, for instance, seems to give insight into the core of who people are. Yet this predilection should be matched by three cautions. First is the risk implied above, that of overestimating the significance of a frame just because it appears more evident or familiar. Being Latino or Korean may matter far less to someone's deep sense of personal authority than being a credentialed professional, for example. Second and related is the reductionistic peril of considering individuals or groups through only one frame. Each person is a complex web of cultural identities, and contextual study must remain open to this entire web as well as those identities that predominate in specific situations. Third, cultural identity should not be simplistically treated as if it emerges and operates in a private enclave. People readily live out these identities in a complex multicultural reality alongside others from whom they differ greatly. This can and often does include significant cross-cultural borrowing and hybridization. Your framing of a group should not be so narrowly inward in focus that it cannot account for this outward intermingling of cultural identities.

With these cautions in mind, you should also be clear about why you are framing your contextual study in this fashion. Surely you will more fully appreciate the stories, symbols, and heritage of cultural worlds that were previously unfamiliar, and this in itself is good. Preachers are prone to a utilitarian tendency at this point, though, in trying to adapt this learning into words and images that make the sermon more appealing. We will return in the final chapter to ways that context can be incorporated into preaching, but for now let us be honest that framing for the sake of superficial appeal is just another means for devaluing and colonizing other cultures, a move that ruptures rather than establishes trust. How and why you frame contextual study therefore has ethical implications. The main reason for framing the cultural identities in a context should be the self-discovery and personal transformation of the preacher, not trying to sound more like those you have studied. Ministers experienced with preaching amidst cultural diversity have often noted this paradoxical outcome. What they gained from other cultures did more to change their own perceptions than it affected sermon style or content.[10]

Frame as Support

A less obvious way we think about a frame is as a structure within something. This is how we speak of the frame inside a wall or building, or the human physique. The composition beneath the surface is central to this use of the term. Although usually hidden from view, this kind of frame is still essential because of its connective strength, giving objects coherence and durability. When turning to the study of context, such framing means to expose the underlying systems of a setting that can help us realize how groups work. It shows us the background to the dynamics in a context, with special attention to organizational behavior. Preachers can therefore find it helpful for trying to clarify what happens in the inner workings of a congregation or its related setting. If you want to engage listeners in terms of their roles and activities in a congregation or somehow affect institutional processes and directions, this kind of framing can help to guide your contextual study.

Instead of focusing us on the cultural characteristics of people (the first category of framing), this approach looks at organizations in a collective fashion. In our case, this usually means looking at congregations, many of whose features can be framed just like any other organization. Leadership consultants Lee Bolman and Terrence Deal use such framing to highlight typical features in organizations that relate to four operational concerns. The *structural frame* foregrounds how things unfold in a group. Assuming that a group is not haphazard but employs rational and coordinated action, this frame makes us aware of its social architecture, the processes, rules, and purposes that give it direction. The *resource frame* attends to what a group has on hand to accomplish its aims. Skills, information, finances, property, and people are central in this frame, which looks at the available goods to be mobilized for perceived needs. The *political frame* identifies who gets things done in a group and their means of doing so. This frame depicts the power relations of a group, including who has voice, when bargaining happens, and how conflict is settled. Finally, the *symbolic frame* brings out why these things matter within a group. Here we get a sense of the meanings and values that are powerful for group identity and direction, which are often carried through channels like story, ritual, and art.[11]

Although preachers may gravitate toward cultural framing in contextual study, many will actually discover that organizational framing grants a more significant understanding of their context. It helps us see the congregation both internally (its operations and subgroups) and externally (its relations to other groups and larger civic life), which is often the most pressing aspect of ministry to engage from the pulpit. This is especially true for preaching insofar as it is a ministry of leadership and formation of the church as a whole, as opposed to an accumulation of otherwise discrete individuals.[12] Group leadership is impeded when problems are misidentified, such as interpreting a power struggle (political issue) as if it were merely a failure to follow the rules (structural issue). It also is stymied when solutions are misapplied, such as consenting to a stewardship campaign treated as a matter of dollars and cents (resource issue) rather than one of faithful witness (symbolic issue). Framing can help ministers appreciate how a congregation systemically implements or avoids its mission. With this awareness, preaching can more directly connect with its context in a way that accurately names existing challenges and effectively sets new direction.

A typical pitfall in framing an organization this way is to look at the context using the frame that is our natural fallback position. By virtue of gifts and training, for example, ministers are quite comfortable seeing the world symbolically in terms of ideals, meanings, interpretation, and hopes. If a disproportionate amount of energy in a setting is expended upon resisting change, however, a symbolic frame will provide some perspective on this (control of this sort is, after all, a strongly symbolic issue), but will miss what a political frame upon the situation could provide. This is exactly why the literature in organizational studies advocates multiple framing and reframing of contexts, to understand the full range of what is at work in a group. To venture further, it may be that such an approach to contextual study will reframe your preaching ministry as well. By moving beyond familiar strategies of analysis, your preaching may in turn become savvy about power or astute about possessions, addressing aspects in the faith lives of listeners that have previously gone undernourished.

Frame as Mind-set

One further way we consider a frame is as an attitude about something. This is how we speak of the frame of reference on a situation, or a mental disposition. The internalized limits and possibilities are significant in this use of the term. When carried within participants, this kind of frame shapes how large or small their world seems to be, including their sense of belonging and agency. Concerning the study of context, such framing means to grasp the multilayered relations in a setting that can help us sense which networks exist. It reveals to us views about connections in a context, with special attention to effective scale. Preachers therefore can find it valuable for trying to make sense of the associations, arrangements, and boundaries that strongly affect how people perceive their ordinary existence. If you hope to engage the diverse levels at which listeners operate in the many ambits of their daily lives, this kind of framing can help to chart your contextual study.

This approach at first may seem the most abstract and least useful way to frame the study of a context. In fact, it refers to the ordinary and thus often overlooked way people perceive themselves to be situated in the world, their internalized sense about what part of that reality matters. We shall speak of this self-locating tendency in terms of the micro, meso (or middle), and macro levels of social interaction:

> Society fits together like a set of nested Russian dolls, with face-to-face interaction constituting the smallest doll in the set. Norms, roles, and statuses are the building blocks of social life. They form the microstructures within which face-to-face interaction takes place. Sustained micro-level interaction is shaped by higher-level structures (sometimes called mesostructures—networks, groups, and organizations). Still larger macrostructures, including classes, states, and systems of patriarchy, constrain the functioning of these networks, groups, and organizations. . . . Big structures thus set limits to our actions. However, it is the small processes of people interpreting, negotiating, and modifying their immediate social settings that gives big structures their dynamism and their life.[13]

Using a *micro frame*, therefore, we notice close relationships and affiliations (such as home, family, and friends). These are included within a *meso frame* that shows the thresholds upon basic public interaction (such as neighborhood, school, and work). These are in turn subsumed into a *macro frame* that reveals the broadest social forces and forms (such as government, economy, and religion). While a person or group lives in all three levels at once, preachers are especially interested in which level makes the most difference and how this perception is reinforced. Framing your contextual study in this way can help you meet listeners where they actually live and suggest ways for them to engage levels other than those they hold most dear.

Another reason this frame is important involves the directional relationship between these levels in daily life, which affects a sense of personal or group power and voice. Some people perceive a bottom-up relationship in which micro forces coalesce to reshape larger levels. This is the interaction of the marketplace, where individual decisions combine into overall trends. Others perceive a top-down relationship in which macro forces impose their will on subsidiary levels. This is the interaction of regulation, where authoritative decisions lead to local compliance. It is therefore not hard to imagine in the former case that people internalize a sense of capability to change their surroundings that is lacking from the more resigned perspective in the latter case. Framing your contextual study in this way can help you become aware of how listeners might respond to a call for action or analysis of social forms and forces at other levels.

A further and often underrated aspect of social life that this frame exposes is the role of the meso level in particular as a place of contact and mediation between the micro and macro. Patterns of human interaction solidify in this middle ground in ways that affect the order and organization of our lives.

For example, micro-level activities and values from our private lives and intimate relations make their impact felt when they are expressed at the meso level. Think of how personal issues influence the workplace, or family life impinges upon volunteer service. Similarly, macro-level forces from systems, nations, and economies significantly structure what meso-level realities can do and how larger forces come to shape our individual lives. Think of how the weight of new laws is felt in schools and neighborhoods, or economic trends redirect available local services. In many ways, the meso level is a crucial first step beyond the private and personal world toward public and civic life, a "mediating institution" that is exceptionally important for all that we do.[14] By contrast, the breakdown or erosion of midlevel groups can produce a fatalistic passivity at the micro level ("What can one person do?"), coupled with an arrogant disconnection at the macro level ("Let them eat cake!"). Framing your contextual study to notice the meso-level can help you see the human networks that contribute to daily life, which in turn has implications for how listeners can or cannot make sense of your preaching.

Relating the Frames

Any of these approaches to framing (as border, support, or mind-set) naturally results in a partial and incomplete view of the context. The same can be said for using any one kind of frame within each approach (such as the class, process, or macro frames). It is worth remembering that the whole purpose of framing is precisely to direct our focus on a few things at a time rather than everything at once. The paradoxical result of this is that the very same context can look quite different depending upon the interests of the one who is observing. Two preachers in a particular setting (whether on the same staff, in separate congregations, or one as successor to the other) will have distinct preaching interests (perhaps faith formation with young adults versus justice for immigrants and refugees) that call for framing their contextual study in quite different ways. In light of these variations, though, how do these two preachers know they have responsibly engaged the same context during the research or from the pulpit? What keeps them from imposing biases that allow them only to see what they want, inventing two disconnected realities out of one local situation?

This concern requires stepping back from the framing process at several points to regain an overall sense of the context. We have already noted the temptation to frame a context only in terms of a few comfortable categories, ways of viewing reality that are already familiar. The real cost of this is not only distorting things to be what you already thought they were but also eliminating any chance to be surprised by and learn from what you discover. From the outset, therefore, you should employ a safeguard known as "triangulation." Regarding frames, this means taking several stances toward the same contextual concern to gain its fullest sense. For example, a study that looks at an ethnically framed challenge might also draw upon the frames of class and belief for complementary perspectives on that concern. Another initial strategy is to adopt an unconventional frame for your research problem. For example, while a societal challenge like health care access might ordinarily be viewed through a macro frame, a micro standpoint could powerfully illumine its impact upon individual lives and families. In a similar way, a study of a congregation's decision making might start from an unusual angle by way of the symbolic frame, rather than the more standard use of political or structural frames.

These two strategies (triangulated frames and unconventional framing) are also valuable once your study is well underway, especially as it changes during the period of research. It may be quite apparent at some point during the process that your research has become stale or stuck, still generating information but without generative insight. At such times, stepping back from your current frames, selecting a new and atypical one, and combining several together can be the key to regaining your momentum. The point is not that contextual study become complicated or lengthy but simply more reliable and accurate.

Using Frames in a Congregation

How would this process look in action? We review now a case study that shows the concepts and strategies of this book in use, one that we will also revisit at the end of the next two chapters. This is no ideal example of perfect planning and research but simply how one pastor came to know his congregational context better and employed those insights in his preaching and other areas of ministry. Based on interviews conducted with the pastor, this case offers only a bare sketch of the rich texture of what he learned. Even so, you might see through his story how a similar process can be workable and valuable in your own setting.

Like many ministers new to a congregation, this pastor encountered a place with rich promise and confusing impressions. He also had a pastoral hunch that something might be amiss, though, and that hunch began with a key—specifically, the key to his office door, of which almost everyone in the congregation had a copy! The pastor's office was treated as public space. In fact, no part of the church building was off-limits or secure, and the same applied to private records and personal materials. The parish secretary was indiscreet with details about church members, gossip was rampant and rewarded, and information was shared in order to secure favor and power. This "open door" policy also had broader consequences. Emotionally freighted behavior was overlooked or excused ("Oh, that's just Bill . . . "), while new ideas quickly became personalized and thus stymied ("I'm *so offended that you . . .*"). The result was paralysis. The most basic decisions by authorized leaders were obsessively micromanaged or simply avoided in order to forestall reactions. People with the worst behavior held the greatest power, controlling programs of the congregation for their own benefit. In the pastor's words, the congregation lost a sense of "appropriateness," of knowing what was fitting for disciples to do as church.

Even lacking further details, this picture may seem quite familiar and clear. Why study this context further? Surely the task should be to resolve the obvious problems. Paradoxically, though, this very impulse gave the pastor pause and drove him to further exploration. He knew he was seeing mainly the negative sides of the most noticeable behavior. Unless, like his predecessors, he was going to retreat into inaction, impose heavy-handed correctives, or give in to the misbehavior, he needed to know more about what was happening at a deeper, theological level of the context. If his hunch was right that the congregation had lost its way about how to be church, then just what kind of church *were* they? How could he begin to appreciate that and engage it honestly? What effect should this then have on his preaching? If sermons are more than weekly group-therapy sessions, what would he actually say? How could he declare good news that his congregants could hear amidst their murky situation?

All of this was at stake for this pastor, grounded in a deep appreciation of these faithful yet flawed people, and it motivated his focus for research. Reflecting on his hunch, he eventually refined something like a research problem. Specifically, he wanted to explore how interpersonal relationships affected ministry patterns in the congregation because these seemed to shape what members thought it meant to be church. This research problem was not driven by general curiosity, however. Instead, his aim was ultimately to gain a better sense of how to proclaim a more life-giving vision for this congregation. By virtue of his calling, he knew he had the time and justification to pursue this study in the ordinary course of his pastoral duties. The advantage of focusing the problem, though, was that it helped him be more selective in the process of contextual study, considering only what pertained to his central concern.

The research question therefore helped him frame what he would or would not explore. Cultural identity (frame as *border*) was perhaps the least helpful for his research, since this group was rather homogeneous in ethnic and other ways. Even so, he sensed that matters of social class played a role in this blue-collar congregation, so he stayed alert for those factors. Far more important was the organizational system (frame as *support*). In terms of Bolman and Deal, he knew that a structural view on the official channels and rules would reveal little. By contrast, a political analysis of how power was used and reinforced, combined with a symbolic awareness of central values and worldviews, were likely the better ways to begin. Finally, thinking about perceived levels (frame as *mind-set*) narrowed his study further. Due to this congregation's apparent fusion, if not confusion, between the micro level (individual and family) and meso level (small group and community), larger social levels would require little or no attention. As noted earlier in this chapter, identifying the most pertinent frames also helped this pastor triangulate his study, using multiple perspectives to assemble a more accurate overall picture.

The reflections we have seen in this case study not only gave direction to the eventual fieldwork (with which the story resumes near the end of the next chapter) but also resulted from a manageable process of thoughtful pastoral reflection. In this pastor's case as well as your own, such reflection is an essential, responsible, caring, and even welcome step. It is, however, only the first step. Framing your study is actually your grounding and backdrop, more of a choreography for research than the actual dance. For those next steps, we turn to the tools that carry you into the frames you have sketched.

Chapter 3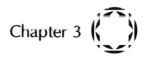

Tools for Exploring Contexts

If you have traced the course of the discussion so far, you may rightly wonder whether a contextual approach to preaching is just too arduous of a path. Perhaps it's not worth the trouble. Surely there is a simpler way. It comes as no surprise that, since this book presents a disciplined range of strategies, all this additional effort is presumed to be good. The real issue, however, is why. As we now introduce a set of tools for studying contexts, it is true that other methods seem initially to be shortcuts. For example, it sounds convenient and orderly to compile statistical data from Web sites about contexts or to design your own survey instruments. Likewise, it appears much easier to read the situational analyses already provided by organizational consultants or social commentators.

It is important to realize, however, that these familiar resources may not deliver what we actually need and might have rather limited value for purposes of preaching. When we try to understand a preaching context and its resident listeners, we seek a personalized, empathetic kind of knowledge. Our goal is not like the naturalist's, seeking empirical information on life-forms or geology in a given, neutral ecology. Nor is ours the statistician's, generating data to be analyzed for its patterns or anomalies. Close as it seems, our aim is not even the anthropologist's, looking at human beings who shape and are shaped by cultural forms. Far beyond facts, ideas, or cultures, we want insight into faithful people and what drives or constrains their faithfulness, especially the transcendent dimension of their lives.

Some research methods and resources are simply not well suited for that aim. Those that reduce living situations to numbers, categories, and typologies are often too abstract for our use, and may overlook how and why people believe as they do. Those that deliver generalities or interpretations at a distance are similarly too remote from actual life settings. Some methods would impose unacceptably high costs of time or other resources in order to amass raw data, let alone make sense of it later. Others require heavy reliance upon supposed expertise or obscure research, evoking a natural level of suspicion or doubt. To be sure, there are highly regarded and readily available social research resources that can, in conjunction with your own contextual study, refine or deepen your local knowledge.[1] Likewise, many fine cultural, social, or historical overviews can connect you to traditions or trends that pertain strongly to your particular setting and without which your insights would be partial or myopic. Even so, these tools by themselves likely cannot provide the contextual study you specifically need as a preacher.

Your preaching context does not consist of numbers or categories but actual listeners: the faithful people who hear you, as well as the worlds in which they make sense of what you say and then, maybe, act upon it. Therefore, we are especially interested in tools that connect us directly to these real people in relation to the concrete, religiously saturated questions or challenges at hand. Since preaching is a rich social practice of group interaction (as noted in chapter 1), the tools we need understandably call for the patience and intentional effort essential to engaging any complex social reality. We already accept that other aspects of pastoral ministry require steady, deliberate attention. Unless your view of pastoral care is advice giving, your form of faith education is information dumping, or your means of worship leadership is agenda management, you know that it takes time and care to learn the complex interpersonal dimensions of these pastoral occasions. No less is true for learning a preaching context. We need reliable, responsible ways to understand that context in both its human scale and holy purpose.

Fortunately, we can turn to the disciplined use of several existing tools in order to support such a careful and caring process of investigation. Best of all, these tools will not require your complete retooling, and may even seem quite familiar. Your own ministerial background likely includes the skills and dispositions for this personal dimension of contextual study. Indeed, your ability to use these tools is probably well in hand, and the time to do so is likely already part of your ministry. In short, we will learn basic strategies for paying attention to your listeners first in terms of their *practices* and then in relation to their *products*. Regarding contextual practices (what people do), we start with the tool of *participant observation*, later augmented by the method of *semistructured interviews*. Regarding contextual products (what people make), we begin with the tool of *artifact and place study*, turning last to the method of *document analysis* to look at one special kind of product.

The sequence for introducing these four tools is not accidental. It might sound more productive to begin with interviews that directly ask what you want to learn. This is the typical approach of journalism or opinion sampling, but it often fails to catch people at work in natural group settings. Similarly, we literate people are quite comfortable scrutinizing documents that contain explicit claims, and therefore prefer to start there. Since only some people's words actually make it into print, however, and even then rather haphazardly, can we really say that a document shows the most important view of a context? In an even greater irony, inexperienced researchers gravitate toward products over practices, so that perceptions of the things people use end up distorting any subsequent encounter with the living people themselves.

In order to gain a more thorough sense of what is happening in a preaching context, therefore, we respect a useful hierarchy in how these tools are usually deployed. Most basic, practices are privileged over products. With practices, participant observation happens first, augmented later by semi-structured interviews. With products, artifact and place study happens first, augmented later by document analysis. In this way, we step back to capture the full, subtle, and complex action of an entire group, reserving more targeted tools (pertaining to interviews or documents) for a later, opportune moment. That said, of course, the responsible discipline in any contextual study is to "triangulate" what we learn, verifying a contextual insight by using different tools from several angles of vision.

Tools That Focus on Practices
Participant Observation
Learning about a human context best begins naturalistically. That is, we try to encounter people doing what they typically would during ordinary interactions in a congregation, such as meetings, rituals, fellowship events, educational opportunities, and so forth. Participant observation is a cluster of strategies (rather than a single technique) for opening up such situations to their full depth. As the name suggests, it involves two components. On the one hand is *participation*, the alert, respectful engagement in activities and events just like any other member of the group. On the other hand is *observation*, paying attention to what people are doing, from the mundane to the extraordinary, as well as how they account for this in their own terms.[2] As a minister, of course, you are not just like any other member, since you have authority and responsibility related to your pastoral call. What is more, you are specifically trying to learn about the context in light of your preaching role. Simply by looking at a group in order to gain contextual insights, you introduce

an aim that others at an event probably do not share. They gather simply to participate, while you are there to learn.

Although you cannot shed your role, knowing and naming it can help you set it aside for a time and become as immersed as you can in an event, just like others. Participation is less about "going under cover" than simply learning to recognize the constraints, opportunities, and relationships that affect anyone in a group. You use all your senses to focus on the whole range of what is happening, and then later try to render an orderly account of what you observed in written form. This written task distinguishes participant observation as a disciplined method. Unlike other folks, you are trying to "take note" in a dual sense, both appreciating what happens and then writing what you discover. Despite this distinctive task, though, participant observation simply activates a well-developed part of your "pastoral mind." Just as you attune all your senses to people and their reactions during a ministry leadership role (such as leading worship, teaching, or running a board meeting), so you engage at this level during participant observation in order more fully to take note of the context.

Using this tool requires advance preparation related to the framing discussion from the preceding chapter. If you framed your work by claiming a research question, selecting a context, and adopting a view of that context that pertains to your driving concern, then you have already begun to identify specific events that merit participant observation. For example, if you want to understand how your preaching can shape a sense of healing in the congregation, participant observation of the Sunday school would probably be less useful than attending a prayer circle or watching how visitation ministers are trained. If you want to know how your preaching intersects with matters of worth and dignity, participant observation at members' workplaces or class interactions during social events are likely to be good targets. In other words, you prepare for participant observation by identifying events most likely to yield insights pertinent to how you framed your research. Learn when and where these events occur, whether you have ready access to them or need special permission to attend, and then consider how you can participate and observe actively yet unobtrusively. Beyond this, you should list beforehand all the topics or concerns you hope to encounter at such an event. Without presuming or limiting what you will discover, think ahead about the areas where special attentiveness is warranted.[3]

With this preparation in place, you are ready to begin the participant observation itself. Since it occurs during an event that unfolds over time, there is a broad chronological pattern to what you are trying to notice. First comes the *arrival threshold*. Events may have a scheduled starting time, but they actually begin in waves. You should therefore arrive well in advance to scope out the overall setting and notice the various participants that arrive at different times and in diverse clusters. This helps you recognize a differentiation in roles, the strong relationships among participants outside the event, and what people symbolize by arriving when they do (such as claims about power or marginalization).

Next comes the *main action* itself. Keep mental track of what happens step by step during the centerpiece of the event, with special attention to a few key questions. Who makes different things happen, from central to peripheral participants? What are people doing in relation to what they are saying? What are the patterns of time in the activity and the centers of gravity in the space? Is there a "script" (like an agenda, timetable, or liturgical order) being followed, and how is it used, enforced, or varied? Are strong symbols being used (perhaps physical objects or even treasured ideas), and who gets to use them for what reasons? Does the event seek to negotiate a change (such as problem-solving or self-improvement), and what are the reactions to this effort? When you pay careful attention to the main action in this way, you will quickly sense how much is happening beyond what ordinary participants usually notice. For this reason, you may wish to jot key observations that will jog your memory when you write detailed notes later.

Finally come the *closure moves*. Even before the scheduled or expected end to an event, you will note that some people are mentally checking out (packing up a briefcase, looking at the clock, and so on). As with arrival, closure happens in waves. Watch who leaves earlier for what reasons, as well as who leaves later accompanied by what further activity. Larger events often break into smaller subgroups and conversation clusters that are important to processing what has just happened. Most pastors are also familiar with the "rump session" or "parking lot committee" that carries the event onward even after it seems to be over. All of these moves toward closure are important for a full understanding of the event you observe.

When the public side of participant observation concludes, your work is by no means over. Even though you will probably be exhausted from paying attention to group interaction, you should begin to write a fuller form of your observations within a few hours of the end of the event. Since electronic recording of events may be inhibiting and ineffective if not prohibited, you must instead rely on your own memory combined with any jotted notes, turning these into a detailed record.[4] This record can appear on a page divided into three columns. A wide central column is for *notations.* Here you describe what was done and said over the course of the event. Particular quotes and significant moments will quickly come to mind while you write, and you should recount these in detail. This column also includes sketches of the spatial arrangement,

locations of people, or major symbols and objects. To the left of these notations is a very narrow column for *indexing*. Here you record a rough time log
of when the events in the central column began or ended, as well as who said
or did various things. The remaining column on the right side of the page is
for *reactions*. During participant observation, you are the main "instrument"
for contextual research. Therefore, your internal questions, emotions, biases,
ideas, and hunches are crucial information to record. Since your study is part
of a ministerial concern about preaching, moreover, theological reflections are
also important. All of these reactions can become the grist for questions you
might pose in subsequent interviews.

As a minister using participant observation, you probably have both wide
access to many events fruitful to study in this way and the freedom to return
to similar events several times over. Having done so, you will have recorded
massive amounts of information. At this point, review your notes carefully for
the topics and insights that help to answer your research question. Trained
researchers do this by "coding" their fieldnotes. They mark when a key term
or topic appears, or when particular people actively contribute to an event.
Although your review probably cannot be this extensive, the broad principles
of coding still apply. Look for the main themes, general patterns, peculiar ruptures, or other features that show significant things happening among those
you observed. Again, not everything in your notes will be of interest but only
those that reveal what you are trying to learn about your preaching context.
Keeping a log of these themes, patterns, ruptures, and features will also be a
good way to know what you should explore using the other tools introduced
in this chapter.

Semi-structured Interviews

Despite a resemblance to ordinary conversation, interviews do not happen
naturally. They are instead artificial events of purposeful, directed dialogue
that treat the respondent's comments as primary information. A built-in tension
therefore exists between the aims of the interviewer and the disclosure by the
respondent. At the same time, interviews are especially well-suited to discovering what is otherwise not apparent by external observation, such as closely
held feelings, values, or memories. For this reason, interviews follow upon what
other tools for contextual study (especially participant observation) notice first.
A further strength about interviews is that they call forth another perceptive
side of your "pastoral mind." Most ministers know the value of basic, authentic
listening in congregational life, especially during pastoral care and counseling.
While an interview does not seek confession or consolation, the experience
of counseling reminds us how quiet attentiveness and carefully chosen words

can open an encounter of profound honesty and trust. These same pastoral abilities come into play when your research includes interviews.

Interviewing actually refers to a continuum of strategies that use different degrees of structure in their design. At one end of this spectrum are "informal unstructured" interviews that try to discover a respondent's views, interests, or concerns in a purely exploratory way, without prepared questions. At the other end are "standardized closed-ended" interviews, with the question sequence set in advance and the available answers restricted to fixed options. For learning about your preaching context, we advocate an approach more in the middle of the range, known as "semi-structured" interviews.[5] This involves developing an agenda or plan of questions linked to your specific research area. The same plan is used in each interview but with considerable flexibility about the sequence or form of the questions and the amount of response generated, depending on how the conversation develops.

For the openness of semi-structured interviews to work well, careful preparation is required. Clarity about your research area will help you focus the *purpose* for interviewing (what you want to learn about the context) and the *sources* you use (those best suited to respond to your questions). With the purpose in mind, you design a list of eight to twelve clear, concrete, open-ended questions that will evoke what you want to know about the preaching context.[6] If designed well, such a list will easily generate an hour or more of conversation. Your list should include a "cross-check" on a key issue (the same question asked two different ways in order to verify a response), and the list usually ends by inviting any further remarks from the respondent. Test the list in a practice session with a mock respondent to see if the questions are clear and have a natural logic or flow. Such practice will also build your familiarity and confidence with the process. Designing this list of questions leads directly into identifying those you will interview. These respondents are contacted in advance to explain the purpose for the interview, detail its conditions (such as length of time or use of results), gain their permission, and arrange its time and place. Finally, assemble what you will need during the interview (like the question list and writing or recording materials) and what you will do if these are missing or fail to work.

Having arrived for the interview as arranged, confirm that your respondent is undistracted and ready. Begin with an appreciative greeting, reminding your respondent about the purpose of your study and any conditions to which you both agreed. The bulk of your time, of course, involves using your list of questions. Earlier practice will help you know the best place to start. At the same time, the conversational flow will suggest an appropriate order to follow, since it is essential only that all of the questions are addressed (even if not overtly asked) during the course of the interview. While the verbal answers to the questions are obviously important, also pay attention to the accompanying emotional tone, subtle body language, and overt gestures or expressions. These observations are often important for grasping what a response means, and so should be noted during the interview. Indeed, even if the interview is recorded, writing notes serves to capture these nonverbals, signal your interest in the conversation, track your personal intuitions and reactions, and monitor your progress through the list of questions (which may take a quite wandering course). Whenever the list of questions seems finished, the interview moves toward closure by thanking the respondent and assuring any promised follow-up contact. Once the formal interview ends, be prepared for an informal period in which "just one more thing" needs to be said. These are sometimes the most important remarks of all.

While the questions you ask give shape to a semi-structured interview, there is also a more subtle activity called "probing." These are your verbal signals during the interview that help the respondent refine or extend what was said but without interruption or overreaction. Six types of probes are natural in this way. *Silence*, simply pausing and waiting, indicates that you are ready to hear more. *Encouragement*, with small affirmations like "uh-huh" or "okay" or "I see," also suggests that a remark could go further. *Elaboration* is a more overt way to do this, specifically by asking for development ("Could you tell me more about . . ."). *Redirection* invites the conversation to turn toward some new aspect, such as asking "where" or "how" or "why" follow-up questions. *Clarification* is perhaps the most directive probe, where you indicate a puzzle or contrast in the interview so far ("What did you mean . . ." or "I don't understand . . ."). Finally, *repetition* allows you to check an earlier response simply by mirroring it back to the respondent ("So you're saying that . . ."). These various probes multiply the depth and impact of the list of questions you brought into the interview.

As with participant observation, you should set aside time soon after a semi-structured interview to review your notes and reflect on what you have learned. Your aim is to elaborate your record, including further recollections and impressions, and to indicate any initial themes or patterns that emerged in the flow of the interview. Once you have completed several interviews using the same list of questions, you can then step back to consider the broader insights you have gained. Were there repeated concerns, topics, expressions, or claims? Were there contradictions or disjunctions between different interviews, or between the words and actions within each interview? Were your questions corrected, redirected, or even avoided? Were particular terms, sayings, or categories used that conveyed a flavor of the local setting?

Were important stories or images used that suggested a broad horizon of meanings or values? Reflecting in this way, you begin to say what you now know from these interviews, how this fills in the picture of your preaching context, and whether this indicates further interviews or other research tools to which you should turn.

As noted earlier in this chapter, our familiarity with interviews may lead us to think they are the best way to garner contextual insights. Semi-structured interviews certainly do afford an active role in pursuing issues, clarifying meanings, and targeting audiences, all while engaging with a wealth of local wisdom. At the same time, such interviews have their weaknesses. They are surprisingly costly in terms of time and labor. If done carelessly, they can generate answers that distort or mask what respondents truly think, or even trigger resistance and hostility. At their best, interviews use the script of questions as a catalyst for a new account that is improvised in the give-and-take between interviewer and respondent, much like a dramatic performance. They do not uncover absolute truth but versions of what people hold to be true, which are in turn compared and checked against versions gained by other tools.

Tools That Focus on Products
Artifact and Place Study

A great deal of what you can learn about your preaching context is found in the overt practices that call for your participation or conversation. Yet much in that context is also latent, discovered in things people make and use that may tell a distinctive story about the situation. The challenge with these things is, of course, their passivity. Such products are actually traces of practices, unable to account directly or fully for themselves. Sometimes you are fortunate enough to encounter them in action, such as sacred objects during ritual, texts while they are written or read, or locales employed in group activities. More often, however, you will come upon products that are silent and at rest, not showing or telling anything under their own power. In these cases, you need to scrutinize and question these products, draw implications about their role or meaning, and explore them further in conjunction with other research tools. Artifact and place study is just such a strategy for enabling these products to convey their own version of the context.[7]

An *artifact* is simply any material object that results from human intention and effort. Materials found in nature are not in themselves artifacts but instead become such through human action. For example, a tree as such is not an artifact. If sawn and planed into boards, however, or if a portion (like a branch) retains its natural appearance but is used ceremonially, the result is treated as an artifact. Considered in this way, the number and range of artifacts throughout your congregation is potentially dizzying. It is impossible and pointless to consider all of them. Instead, you focus only on those artifacts most significant to informing what you want to learn about your preaching context.

A *place* is just a special kind of artifact with three distinct features. First, a place has greater scale than an artifact. Outwardly it interacts with the surrounding environment, while inwardly it serves as a container for human practices and products. Place therefore implies notions of boundary and location in a way an artifact does not. Second, a place involves many more structurally interacting components than an artifact. There is often great complexity in this overall arrangement, so that altering just a few components radically changes how the system of a place works or what it means. Third, a place confers intentional meaning upon a given space and everything within that area. Its scale and complexity constitute a symbolic reality that lends significance to whatever happens or is located in that place.

Since artifacts and places are similar and interact with each other, we can use the same strategies to understand them better. This begins with recognizing that they fall into a few broad categories, which in turn reveal the special challenges in studying them accurately. Some are *self-interpreted*. Artifacts or places may have textual labels that overtly declare a purpose (like signs posted in a church kitchen), or they are so narrow in use that the purpose is relatively clear (like a baptismal font). Of course, anything in this category may still be adapted later to other uses. Other artifacts or places are *intentionally ambiguous*. For example, an artist may create a work with multiple meanings irreducible to just one. Similarly, strong and highly charged symbolic objects (like water or flame when used in worship) may bear many meanings at once and resist being contained. Another category includes artifacts or places that are *reappropriated*. Imagine that the original purpose for some product has diminished or became obsolete (such as a mimeograph machine) or perhaps faced some crisis or rejection (such as the location for an American flag). In such cases, artifacts or places may later be reclaimed with deeper historic, symbolic, or affective values than ever before (which is why churches find it so hard to dispose of anything). Finally, artifacts or places sometimes have an *unknown use*. Especially in a new situation, the meaning people give to an object or location may seem veiled and mysterious. Some sort of guide or "culture broker" can open the door to whether this mystery is the result of amnesia, disconnection from the original users, or an effort to mask meanings from outsiders.

With these categories in mind, you begin by focusing on a particular artifact in its usual "home" or discerning a place that merits closer attention.

The study then involves posing a series of questions about the material data, which should include at least six interrelated aspects:

1. *History*—When did the artifact or place originate? What have been its subsequent periods of greater or lesser use?
2. *Setting*—What is the typical environment for the artifact or place? How is it embedded there as part of an ensemble of other artifacts or places?
3. *Users*—Who were the original creators of the artifact or place? Who have been the main or authorized users since then?
4. *Technology*—What were the materials, labor, and design involved in creating the artifact or place? What skills or abilities are needed for its continued use?
5. *Function*—What were the original purposes for the artifact or place, both intended and actual? How have these shifted or been augmented or diminished since then?
6. *Meaning*—What significance or narrative is carried by the artifact or place? Is its meaning primarily functional, aesthetic, symbolic, or something else besides?[8]

In posing these questions, you maintain a written log of your answers and the ways you reached them, especially the people or materials that served as informing sources. Indeed, many of these questions will call for using other tools from this chapter, such as conducting interviews, observing key events, or reviewing written records. In any case, at a later point your log can be labeled to highlight themes, topics, or other valuable insights that pertain to your contextual interest and can be compared to what you have learned by other means. As you can see, the use of this strategy is not as sequential as tools that focus on practices, which follow a natural progression of before, during, and after. By contrast, this kind of tool demands that you carefully reflect on the artifact or place in its own right. It therefore brings out a different side of your "pastoral mind." Over time, you have likely developed a sensitivity to how ministry is shaped by the space and surroundings in which it happens. For example, you may arrange a room and its furnishings in one way for a Bible study, another way for a wake, and yet another for a committee meeting. The skill you bring to artifact and place study is this deep and almost intuitive awareness that "stuff matters." Drawing upon this will help you hear what material objects and environments can say about your preaching context.

Document Analysis

Though we rarely consider it, documents are also artifacts. They are distinctive by their central use of symbols meaningful in a language (words, numbers, or other figures) produced in material media by some kind of technology (writing, print, images, and so on). In short, they primarily involve texts.[9] Because they express meaning in language and because language evokes its own world, we can easily imagine documents offer a self-contained language world available simply by reading. This is why we stress that they are also artifacts, products of and for human use, and therefore embedded in and reflective of actual contexts. In other words, document analysis calls for noticing the interaction between the *meanings within* documents and the *settings beyond* them.[10] As a resource for understanding contexts, documents must themselves be understood contextually. This should come as no surprise, however, since your "pastoral mind" is already acquainted with sleuthing through texts to listen for how a story from the past may connect with people yet today, whether those texts take the form of church histories, financial records, or sacred Scriptures.

Before you examine documents, reflecting on a few questions will save you considerable time. First and foremost, how will these documents inform you about your preaching context? Within one document or across a collection, which portions will be most useful to your research question? Do you seek documents for exploration (to shape hunches or generate ideas) or for evidence (to support a claim or show a contrast)? Do you think they will mean just what they say (reflecting an actual reality in the world), more than what they say (offering many layers to grasp), or other than what they say (exposing power or ideologies)? Failure to clarify these matters beforehand may lead to document analysis that is wandering and wasteful.

One other orientation is helpful. Documents are broadly categorized by their origins and purposes. In terms of *origins*, the question is whether a document's authorship is primary (eye witness to the events presented), secondary (someone from a later time), or tertiary (a summary of secondary accounts). In addition, a document may have been solicited by an outside request (like surveys) or unsolicited because of innate interests (like diaries). In terms of *purposes*, the question is whether a document's production is "for a place" (institutional records and histories), "in the world" (public texts and data), or "of a life" (personal letters and accounts). These purposes connect with availability, which ranges from closed (classified items) to restricted (medical records) to archival (census materials) to published (news reports). The reason to recognize these categories is to discern the value of a document as a source of information. As a rule of thumb, a document is more valuable when its production is closer to the time and place of the events it presents, and its form is closer to the original version.[11]

With this orientation, you can begin *accessing* documents, which usually happens in four steps. First, you identify which documents or parts thereof are relevant for your purposes. Next, you locate where these documents are available (personal or public collections) and how they are arranged (from haphazard to catalogued). Then you select those materials you can reasonably hope to examine, using an appropriate sampling method. Finally, you collect these materials for examination on site, borrowing off-site, duplication, or reproduction. For example, I once was trying to understand better how one congregation's musical life contributed to its current sense of identity. The monthly newsletter was one crucial resource for this purpose since it meticulously recorded the hymn selections for every worship service. Surprisingly, the church office had no centralized file of these newsletters, but I learned that a few longtime members retained copies in their homes. Indeed, one of them could have provided newsletters stretching back for decades, far more data than I needed. As a result, I borrowed only the five most recent years from her collection, copied the relevant portions about hymns, and returned them later.

With the materials in hand (whether originals, a copy, or detailed notes), you turn to *evaluating* documents, which involves two steps. The first is description, which records all the features of the document that might matter to your study. This can include the literary type or genre, the physical condition or appearance, the history and location of both the authorship and the production, information about why and for whom it was written, the content (including any problems with understanding it), alternative versions, and so forth. While some of these initially seem irrelevant to your interests, you may be surprised at their significance when you combine them with insights gained by other tools. With the newsletters mentioned above, for example, the history of who wrote those hymn records and why told a great deal about the ethos of the congregation. After description, the second evaluation step is appraisal, which looks at the quality of the document. Your concern here is whether the document is both authentic and representative. Is it reliably what it claims to be, or has it been changed or even distorted? Does it resemble other documents of its type and relate to its subject matter in a credible way? It is not hard to imagine how important these questions are when listening to the story that financial records can tell, let alone many other kinds of material.

Accessing and evaluating documents leads to the ultimate aim of document analysis, *interpreting* them. We noted earlier that because they are artifacts, documents convey meanings within and settings beyond themselves.

These same two relationships come into play during interpretation. Referring to the "meanings within" (the language world of the document itself), several sorts of review are possible. Content analysis looks for the repetitions, key terms, and dominant themes, while discourse analysis looks for the style, literary forms, and broad structure. Alternatively, the surface clarity (what is plain versus what is obscure) can be contrasted with the underlying substance (implicit values, issues, or tensions). Referring to the "settings beyond" (the larger world of the document's origins and use), one approach is to explore the document's point of view within its original environment. Another is to look instead at the changing role the document had in later situations that impinge upon your contextual interest. All told, these interpretations help you notice similarities to or differences from what you have learned using other tools, corroborating your insights or complicating what once seemed simple.

Using Tools in a Congregation

We return now to the case study introduced near the end of the last chapter in order to see how the pastor we met there moved from framing his research toward using fieldwork tools. You may recall that the pastor's hunch was that his congregation had a weak sense of appropriate boundaries and behaviors, which stymied its faithful discipleship. In particular, he wanted to know better how interpersonal relationships affected ministry patterns and how that in turn shaped what it meant for them to be church. In preparation for contextual study in light of that focus, he framed his research further by deciding to look especially at the power use and dominant values of the group (political and symbolic frames) and how domestic and congregational life were virtually merged (micro and meso frames). To a lesser extent, he also wanted to keep in mind how class identity contributed to the overall situation.

What happened next was both ordinary and exceptional. Without significant changes to his usual schedule or workload, this pastor used the ordinary, natural interactions of his ministry as the main places to begin the fieldwork. The exceptional dimension was that he did so with new purpose and energy, using the tools introduced in this chapter to direct his learning and address the research problem. He admitted that he did not develop in advance a step-by-step plan for which tools he would use when but was more opportunistic in much of his study. Over the course of several months, he simply recognized instances that related directly to the research problem as he had framed it, and then adopted the fitting tools that could discipline his study at those points.[12] Near the end of his investigation, he was surprised to realize he had used every tool at his disposal to one degree or another, although some were less useful in light of his main focus. The following sketch touches on several highlights of his study. To reinforce your own learning, this sketch follows the order in which the tools were introduced in this chapter rather than the sequence of the pastor's fieldwork.

Participant observation of ordinary church council and committee meetings proved to be immediately accessible and profoundly fruitful. Rather than simply following along with the apparent purpose of these events, the pastor began to notice the subtle cues and interactions in the background. Council meetings were conducted as if in a living room. Casually seated on couches rather than more formally around a table, leaders repeatedly engaged in lengthy periods of reporting on individual lives and personal news. Committee meetings centered on close relationships as well. This was especially apparent during strong emotional reactions against new ideas because, for example, a relative of a committee member might be hurt. Participant observation was also useful for noticing the close affiliations between those who frequently stopped by the church office for no particular reason, as well as how a period for welcoming newcomers during worship had actually become a time to greet relatives and old friends. In the end, this tool helped the pastor to learn the profound level of relationship maintenance and protection built into the core of how this congregation acted.

Semi-structured interviews were also valuable but required the greatest intentional departure from the pastor's routine. Knowing that information was power in this congregation, he began by inviting current and recent officers to tell him what he didn't yet know, the important stories they thought he ought to hear. Similar questions were posed of neighboring ministers familiar with the congregation, as well as (in a less structured casual way) of long-standing members who were now shut-ins. Perhaps most distinctively, the pastor conducted a series of group interviews in a "cottage meeting" format. Three simple questions guided these sessions: "What do you love about our church?" "What do people say about us now?" and "What do you hope for our future?" As people learned that the pastor was listening carefully, he found he rarely needed to set up further interviews. Members would instead just drop by, wanting to tell their stories and share their perspectives. In the end, this tool helped the pastor learn both the meaning of and mood about church, especially how members feared that the congregation's best days were over, replaced by a grim and frightened determination to survive.

Artifact and place study was the tool that most surprised this pastor for what it revealed. Time and again, he learned that common objects, some regularly used and some long ignored, were actually placeholders for people. Lay leaders used treasured worship materials in ways that imitated a beloved pastor from long ago rather than reflecting typical practices of their denomination.

Dusty, untouched file cabinets were filled with three decades of meticulous Sunday school lessons drafted by a teacher who had died years before. A wall of photographs honoring previous pastors strategically omitted those held in ill repute, while one important room in the building was named in honor of a powerful member widely known to have been difficult and unethical. The congregation's nearby cemetery was more important for being the private turf of those who tended it than for the deceased members buried there. In the end, this tool helped the pastor learn how the prized goods and special spaces memorialized a particular, enmeshed history of involvement in this congregation, one that was highly selective and tightly controlled.

Document analysis was perhaps the least useful tool for informing the pastor's contextual study, contrary to his initial expectations. To be sure, a few valuable insights came from various church histories as well as the pattern of information recorded in the monthly newsletter. More revealing, however, was the simple absence of key texts. For example, church records about baptisms, weddings, funerals, and membership had not been accurately updated in many years, on the grounds that, "We all know what happened." The paucity of written information led the pastor to an innovative strategy. As part of the annual stewardship drive, he asked members to submit brief stories about the place of the congregation in their faith lives. Responses were so numerous that the results were later copied and distributed for all to read. As a whole, the booklet of these stories revealed a fascinating pattern. Nearly half of the stories recounted some version of, "My family and friends are in this congregation, and so God is active in this place," while an almost equal number of the rest shared an account like, "Something unexplainable happened to me personally, and so God is active in my life." In the end, this tool helped the pastor learn that the faith expressions of members were highly privatized, centering mostly on strong interpersonal relationships and the solitary interior life.

As this pastor's fieldwork wound down, he was left to sort through a dizzying array of insights about roles, relationships, power, and commitments. In time, however, something more came into focus. Careful study had led him to a profound awareness of the remarkably close bonds in the congregation that had become an end unto themselves. Since these bonds were so significant to the personal lives of members, they had to be nurtured and protected at all costs, even if they were sometimes burdensome and impeded the congregation's ministry. The pastor now glimpsed a paradox: the congregation these bonds were intended to sustain and on which it relied so heavily was now endangered by them. When this case study resumes near the end of the next chapter, we will trace the move from such initial fieldwork insights to what they might more fully mean. For now, however, if you are reasonably disciplined in using all four tools in this chapter (like the pastor in this case study), you will already begin to see your own setting in new ways. What you still lack, though, is a way to employ those insights toward proclamation. The power of what you have learned now must be channeled toward its appropriate role for your preaching. Moving toward that aim is our remaining challenge in knowing the context.

Chapter 4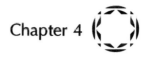

Signs for Interpreting Contexts

By now, you have surely learned a great deal about your situation. Some insights have simply confirmed your hunches. Others were remarkable, even confounding. As a preacher, though, what do you do with this? Be assured, your research has already begun to change your preaching at a subterranean level. For one thing, you are affected by and alert to the context in new ways. Increased access to practices and products attunes you to local conditions. Besides this, the process of contextual study quickly exposes your own social placement in the setting, awareness of which shapes your character as a preacher. Finally, your research builds up social and pastoral capital in the congregation. Due to your efforts, people in the congregation now know you are listening to them, which predisposes them to hear you more closely as well.

Beneficial as these are, they are incidental and sporadic outcomes. Our main task in this chapter is to marshal what you have learned toward an intentional and sustained approach to contextual preaching. The key to this process comes in realizing that you have done much more than amass information about your particular situation. Such information has its place, of course, granting orientation and basic comprehension, but it is a modest role. Far more than facts, you are gradually developing a sense of the *signs* in your congregation. These are the markers of what matters seriously, what bears greatest meaning, and what conveys ultimate claims, transcendent realities, or even genuine holiness. In turning now to signs, we resume a topic first mentioned in chapter 1. At that point, we noted that because preaching is cultural, it can attend to context by being a symbolic word. Signs are exactly the means by which we recognize the symbolic freight of a local setting, name more aptly what is important there, and then interact with a context's profound cultural resources through what we proclaim.

We begin with a basic introduction to signs as a way to interpret what your fieldwork has uncovered. In the course of this introduction, two different but related categories of signs are elaborated. While both are valuable for our purposes, one is favored for its special role in linking what you have learned in your research with what you will say in your preaching, and therefore receives extended attention. Even so, this chapter only explores how signs help you understand what is at stake for a *local context* of preaching. There remains the further question of how this can or should relate to what is at stake for a *scriptural text* in preaching. Although we enter upon that longer trajectory here, its completion must await the final chapter.

Signs and What They Mean

Even more than the frames and tools encountered in previous chapters, the background scholarship about signs belongs to a massive and technical academic literature.[1] Venturing into this terrain is therefore fraught with perils of imprecision and oversimplification. Yet familiarity with the entire field of semiotics is not required to learn the generally accepted concepts essential for a basic grasp of what signs are and how they work. Signs are not some further element "out there" in your preaching context waiting to be discovered by additional fieldwork. Instead, the task now involves making sense of what you have already learned and thereby beginning to interpret it more authentically. Looking beyond our conventional perceptions is not without effort, however. It requires that we first embark on a modest side-trip into the conceptual world of signs, one that calls for patience. At the same time, attention to these concepts is no recent trend imposed on preaching in order to make it sound theoretically respectable. Using signs to interpret our world has been a homiletical concern since the time of Augustine, if not even earlier.[2] In turning to signs, preachers renew an ancient and venerable acquaintance.

Simply put, a sign happens when anything is culturally taken to represent something else. As a result, there are three components to a sign: the form it has in the world (technically, the *signifier*), the meaning to which it relates (the *signified*), and the way these two are linked (the *signification*).[3] For example, written letters and words in an alphabetic language (like those on this page) stand for vocal sounds and vocabulary concepts. A person's facial expressions can be seen as expressing moods and emotions. The size and condition of a house may be taken as an indicator of social or economic status. Noticing signs therefore involves a special double-gaze of *both* the form of the sign on its own *and* the meaning or reality to which it gestures.[4]

The challenge is to grasp appropriate connections between a sign's form and meaning, as well as the depth of relationship between the two, a challenge with the potential for ambiguity and confusion. It is therefore important to notice in our examples how culturally embedded the link truly is between a sign's form and meaning. Even something as straightforward as a smile or frown is associated with specific emotions due to our own cultural perspective, which often becomes evident only when, in a very different milieu, we fail to grasp the sinister intent of a smile or the playful connotations of a frown. Knowing how signs work is therefore important precisely because of the extent and complexity of these meanings in your preaching context. In light of what you have already learned using various tools, you now need to ask further what these insights might really mean and at what levels of reality. Discernment of signs provides just such an interpretive strategy.

The basic distinction between a sign's form and meaning now lets us explore more thoroughly how these two are connected. Signs can be arranged along a continuum anchored at each end by quite different relationships between form and meaning. At one end are *indexical* signs, referring to how the form of a sign simply marks or "indexes" its conceptual value. A gravestone in a cemetery is an indexical sign. Its location correlates to a buried body, for which it also provides basic facts like name and lifespan. The form of an indexical sign stands for or points to its meaning, which is often apparent, uncomplicated, and descriptive. At the other end of the spectrum are *iconic* signs, referring to how the form of a sign enables participation in its conceptual value, as when Orthodox Christians treat certain paintings as windows or "icons" of divine reality. Reading a story or listening to music can be iconic signs. Their enactment produces the experience intended by the author or composer, and often leads to entering the deep reality performed by way of words or notes. The form of an iconic sign engages and shares in the heart of its meaning, which is usually condensed, complex, and in need of explication.[5]

Indexical and iconic signs are not mentioned so we can create separate abstract categories. Instead, we want to point out the increasing depth at which some signs in our everyday lives operate and the extent to which we must go if we would understand them fully. Consider the sign of two people holding hands. In its simplest form, this sign can be viewed indexically. It marks or indicates a relationship between these people. What that relationship is may initially be unclear (for example, whether it is friendship, romance, or assistance), but at the least it indexes a level of intimacy where such physical contact is fitting. Is that all there is to hand-holding as a sign? Surely it would be superficial to stop there. At the more iconic end of the spectrum, we can begin to sense how much more is involved in this practice. To hold the hand of another person not only shows that a relationship exists but also how doing so enacts that relationship. People in love do not just happen to hold hands, of course, but act this way because it is part of what it means to be romantic. In other words, if we would understand this sign truly, then hand-holding must be pressed as far as possible beyond the merely indexical (what the sign shows to others) to the fully iconic (what the sign performs for users).

Shift the example now to something you may have noticed about your preaching context. Consider the sign of the congregation when it gathers. At an indexical level, that sign simply marks an activity of the group as part of its life. People in churches occasionally assemble, and we just associate this with what congregations ordinarily do. Is that all there is to gathering as a sign? Taken more iconically, we might instead ask what gathering discloses about actually being church. At this level of interpretation, a deeper significance becomes apparent. To gather is not simply a sociological coincidence but an active statement of meaning. For one thing, it says that Christian faithfulness is not sufficiently embodied in isolated living. Believers gather as a way of being fully human in the image of God, sharing with others as body of Christ, supporting one another as sisters and brothers. Moreover, other practices that accompany the sign of gathering (singing, praying, listening, eating, washing, and so forth) further embellish the full value of this sign at the iconic level. To enact this entire, rich sign is something like what believers suspect it means to be part of God's household, sharing in abundant life that exceeds the apparent limits of everyday existence. The point is that we fail to understand this sign of the gathered congregation until we move toward the iconic dimension: not simply what the sign means about us but how we participate meaningfully through it.

Such an example is perhaps a bit ideal, and of course not everything you discovered in your contextual study can be pressed to such an iconic level of interpretation. Some things you encountered may have been truly interesting, but even so, their value remains mostly indexical. Such signs are certainly also important for contextually attuned preaching because they mark out the broad features of the symbolic landscape. Our central interest, however, will be to pursue especially those insights that you already sense will hold a greater iconic significance. These are the signs you can appreciate first in an indexical way (what they simply say and demarcate) but then investigate further for their further iconic qualities (how they enable participation in something more). Recognizing local insights as signs in their full range of meanings is ultimately what helps preaching to speak more amply in a context.

Strong Signs as the Focus

During this side-trip into the ambit of signs, we first distinguished a sign's form in the world from the meaning to which it relates, and then how such meaning can be interpreted not only indexically but also, in certain cases, iconically. To extend this journey another step, we should reflect a bit more closely on why certain signs, when interpreted iconically, manifest an unusual level of depth and significance. It takes little effort to bring to mind such strong signs from within our own familiar settings. All the more remarkable, however, are those signs that speak far beyond their cultural home or period and yet exert a profound impact upon us. You enter a cathedral or mosque built centuries ago and are still overcome with awe. You hear prayers or chants from an unfamiliar tradition and nonetheless become deeply reflective. Why does this happen with some signs and not others? To grasp this is crucial to our focus in this book, since these strong signs are precisely what contextually astute preaching tries to engage.

Historian of religion Mircea Eliade provided a useful account of such signs (which he called "symbols").[6] He first observed that a symbol originates in an actual situation where it has concrete value and use. As the symbol takes on greater and greater significance, however, those origins are not erased or minimized but subsumed into its expanding value. For example, think of a family heirloom like an antique platter reserved only for holidays. Although gradually associated with treasured memories and meals, these later develop-ments never change the fact that it once was an ordinary dish that could still function in that way today. The difference is that the subsequent process of symbolization has added further meanings to the original form. In a sense, it is no longer relegated to its initial reality alone (meal practices) but now connects with a much larger system of meanings (family identity and belonging). Strong signs are distinctive, therefore, because they are first of all embedded in and refer to a larger structure and history of significance, including their connec-tions with other strong signs.

Another way to explain the power of strong signs is that they suggest universal realities of existence. Beyond mundane or ordinary matters, they refer to the most potent and prevalent dimensions of the human condition. For example, I once studied a congregation in which many practices rein-forced a general motif of "order." Everything from conduct during meetings to dutiful work habits to widely shared expectations to sanctions against disruption were part of the orderly ethos of this congregation. These were more than isolated or haphazard instances, however. Taken together, they evoked a fundamental human anxiety to avoid chaos and uncertainty, a mat-ter especially (but not strictly) acute in this small, struggling congregation.

Eliade noted that symbols usually address just such "limit situations" of life: fear and hope, desire and relief, and the many other parts of life that elude a rational or empirical grasp.

Strong signs also work by expressing deep truths in a way that natural phenomena simply cannot. They quite often incorporate the two sides of a tension or paradox, both of which must be held together if we want to express the true richness of life. As products of cultural meaning-making, strong signs achieve this in a way that is not available within the bare reality of the ordinary world. Consider the familiar case of church members who commit to build homes for those without adequate housing. As we have already noted, the sign involved is not only a structure for living (basic, original level) but also participates in a larger system of meaning (shelter or neighborhood). In addition, the sign becomes yet more profound because it suggests the common human longing for home, safety, and thriving. Yet this sign is not uncomplicated or relentlessly positive. If housing is needed and must be built, this implicitly admits an opposite reality, that it is unavailable for some and would remain so without this special effort. The sign of housing is as much a statement of absence and breakdown as of provision and empowerment. By marrying both sides of this paradox, a symbol speaks with greater strength.

One last aspect of strong signs comes to us not by way of Eliade but Rudolf Bultmann. In a passing comment about the seemingly trivial use of candles at Christmas, he remarked that "the splendor of the light not only makes us happy in an aesthetic and sentimental sense, but rather, as a symbol, has something to say to us—is, so to speak, a word addressed to us."[7] We have already stated that signs carry the cultural meanings we ascribe to them. Bultmann went a step further to venture that strong signs are actually a two-way disclosure. Every such sign conveys not only something *about* us but *to* us as well. At its heart, a strong sign embodies a message we are bid to receive from a source other than ourselves. That is, it bears divine self-disclosure. In relation to contextual preaching, this may be the most important aspect of strong signs for us to notice.

We have taken this extra step toward naming these four features because the real aim for fieldwork is to focus on and name the strong signs that are most revealing about the preaching context. Based on the discussion of signs so far, this involves the relatively simple process of narrowing. You begin by interpreting the insights gathered through fieldwork in order to identify the various available indexical signs. What they disclose may be fairly modest, but at least you begin to appreciate the symbolic contours of the local terrain. This is revealing as far as it goes, but still incomplete. You will likely sense that some of these indexical signs can be pressed further to an iconic level, how they open up participation in the deeper and especially theological levels of the situation. Even here you are not quite done, for the final task is to ask which of these iconic signs are especially strong instances, reflecting on the four features we just reviewed in this section. Which signs are embedded in larger systems of meaning, refer to universal realities of existence, involve multiple and even paradoxical claims, or serve as a means by which a word is addressed to us? A very good test for this comes by noticing those practices and products in your fieldwork that were widely used or mentioned, required a significant outlay of energy or resources, involved unusual or counterintuitive behavior, or became a focus for devotional or reverent attention. You will usually find that when you cluster together those kinds of practices and products, you have probably begun to expose strong iconic signs that can interpret your context in profound ways.

Telling the Truth through Signs

The skeptical or weary might again wonder at this point about the further interpretive move that signs require. Surely our preaching could just sprinkle in a few concepts gleaned through fieldwork and be sufficiently attuned to the setting. In fact, though, the result would be only superficially contextual. At its best, such preaching simply turns the context into a topic or theme to address. The local situation supplies the preacher with fodder for analysis that usually leads to giving advice. At its worst, this approach crassly excavates the context for appealing gems. The preacher uses the local situation to wink at the listener in a bid to be relevant, entertaining, or accepted. Either way, superficially contextual preaching trivializes the actual setting by failing to engage it completely, including theologically. On the one hand, it lacks compassion, sharing fully in our mutual predicament, while on the other, it lacks gravity, declaring God's ways for us that would not otherwise be heard. This happens because of a failure to appreciate signs that become apparent to us only through careful contextual study.

Contextual preaching relies upon and uses signs because it actually aims to tell the whole truth of who we are *coram Deo*, before God. It is still remarkably powerful when a preacher "calls the thing what it actually is."[8] Signs enable precisely this sort of truth telling. What we ultimately need is the capacity to tell the deeper theological truths of a setting, the truths that strong iconic signs are able to disclose. What is more, such signs can then engage the deeper truths of the wider tradition in which we stand. As we will see in the next chapter, our honesty about the preaching context also drives us into a longstanding and ongoing conversation, a critical dialogue with scriptural texts that authorize our proclamation in the church. For the remainder of this chapter, however, we focus directly on the ways that the strongest signs can help us make sense of our context on its own terms, both within and beyond the pulpit.

Suppose that, following the procedure sketched at the end of the preceding section, you interpreted the insights from your context and focused on its strongest signs. It then becomes especially potent for your ministry and preaching to realize how these signs enable truth telling in two broad and compelling ways. On the one hand, they can work like a mirror that reflects us, as participants in a context, back to ourselves. They expose our existence in itself, especially when left to its own devices: limits and capacities, failures and successes, evils and virtues. This use of signs is *indicative*, showing us authentically and recognizably what *already is*. On the other hand, signs can work like a window that affords a glimpse onto something beyond us, even those transcendent dimensions of our lives in a context. They reveal our existence beyond its present confines, especially how it looks in and through God's ways for us. This use of signs is *subjunctive*, showing us faithfully and hopefully what *might yet be*. We turn now to each way that signs tell the truth, both laying bare our old perceptions and opening us onto new vistas.

Sign as Mirror

First, signs serve as a *mirror* of reality by telling a truth that we may not yet realize or perhaps even wish to avoid yet must acknowledge for the sake of abundant life. Recall from chapter 1, however, that the contemporary use of language presents serious problems to those who try to speak honestly. Distorted language evokes a fixation on ourselves, detachment from others, and shallowness about our common plight. As a result, we are quite skillful at using well-developed defenses to block any direct efforts to name who we are. Truth telling therefore faces a basic resistance and may never be heard. How can we overcome this so that people can actually acknowledge and even affirm an honest reflection of themselves? Strong iconic signs are able to do this because they can pursue an indirect route to truths in several different ways.[9]

Sometimes, signs interpret the context by virtue of being *partial*. Seeing a full-scale reflection of a context can be overwhelming. Certain signs avoid this problem by being limited to just a manageable glimpse of the setting. They use a portion to speak of larger and potentially numbing realities. This small patch of the wider landscape creates a place to stand, an initial perspective on broader truths in that context. For example, I once worked with a congregation that perceived a loss of purpose and distinctiveness in its community. A mood of inadequacy was pervasive and paralyzing. What I gradually learned, however, were the many small ways they indeed exercised profound forms of ministry that truly set them apart. Since the congregation despaired at the overall picture they imagined, I invited them to look closely at just one piece of their life. That partial sign was an annual fall dinner they sponsored for the community. It was a remarkable time of serving others, listening for concerns, welcoming strangers, passing on traditions, and teaching leadership to youth. That one strong sign was a microcosm of who they were and helped them claim a greater truth of their place in that community.

A different way signs move past our defenses is to amplify *contrasts*. Congregations tend to segment and separate very different parts of their life for the sake of harmony and stability. A way to break through this is by holding together two or more strong signs that might otherwise remain apart. By doing so, a new question is posed: What do these contrasting truths, when held together, say about us? Several years ago, I studied a congregation that took justifiable pride in being a "family church." They embodied that value in deep care for one another, commitment to home and family as the site of faith formation, and even a ritual "family circle" that concluded worship every Sunday worship. All by itself, that strong sign was a dominant and quite positive image. What it repressed were two other strong signs. The one was an older member's tyrannical behavior in church life, while the other was the congregation's total disconnect from its own neighborhood. When these signs were contrasted, members began to examine a picture of family marred by misconduct within their walls and disregard beyond them. It led to a deeper recognition of what family truly meant, including its limitations and responsibilities.

One other way strong signs can reflect who we are happens by *reacquainting*. It is very easy for congregations to become jaded and tired, unable to appreciate their most remarkable or troubling features. Handled artfully, however, strong signs can cut through this fog and awaken us to what presently seems stale and ordinary.[10] They introduce us to our context in a fresh way, newly aware of its full significance. Some time ago, I spent time with a rural congregation that, through the years, had taken its unusual history for granted. Faced with dwindling membership and programs, they now only saw themselves as depleted. A thorough review of their records, however, revealed remarkable traits they rarely celebrated. For generations, they had raised up a large number of pastors disproportionate for a congregation of their size. They were consistently the first in their area to adopt the denomination's latest hymnal and learn every hymn therein. They continued to sponsor missionaries and seminary students who had no links to their community. When this remarkable treasure was finally dusted off and noticed once more, they could freshly appreciate these deep commitments as a resource for engaging their context anew.

Sign as Window

The other main form of truth telling through signs is using them as a *window* onto what might yet be. The challenge to overcome in this case, however, is not defensiveness. Instead, it is shortsightedness, a lack of imagination that entraps people in fatalism about their context. Truth telling therefore faces a basic despair that may obstruct efforts to change. How can we overcome this in order to reclaim a sense of hope and future, even a vision of participating in God's ways? Strong iconic signs are able to do this because they can redirect us beyond conventional ways of looking at the situation. Again, this happens in several ways.

One approach is to notice signs that provide *gestures*. Sociologist Peter Berger claims there are certain traits within ordinary human behavior that point beyond the empirical to a transcendent reality. He refers to these as "proto-typical human gestures," commonplace acts and experiences that express essential claims and orient human existence.[11] Strong signs can sometimes be used in this way, identifying practices that gesture at deeper concerns about limits, failure, meaning, or hope. Concretely, this calls for looking at those times when, even in small ways, people refuse to accept the given terms of their context as final. For example, periods of play create an alternative reality amidst mundane structures, while forms of humor use irony or reversal to resist a dominant interpretation. By contrast, lament and even outrage are significant because they show that a line of harm or injustice has been crossed and therefore demands strong response. Other such gestures can be imagined, but their importance is in giving us a view of the orienting commitments in the local reality that suggest still deeper values and claims. Noticing these can stimulate people to consider alternative ways of being and acting.

A different tactic is to use signs that create *reconnection*. Being isolated and left to our own devices often obstructs our imagination about who we might yet be. Some signs, especially narrative forms, can be powerful ways to repair that isolation by linking the local story to a larger, life-giving discourse. A study team I knew looked at a Roman Catholic parish composed of two ethnic groups sharply at odds. An uneasy truce allowed each to claim a separate Sunday mass as its own. The implications of this were troubling, but no one could see a way beyond the impasse. During a meeting about the dispute, however, a member began to tell a story about the processional cross. Instead of being a typical crucifix, it incorporated an empty space shaped like a human body. This man admitted that when he looked at that cross, he tried to imagine his enemies within that space as people Jesus also loved, even unto death. That simple link between the local dispute and the passion narrative dramatically changed the conversation. The image was frequently mentioned during the continued efforts toward reconciliation. As a strong sign, it opened a new way to look beyond the present entrenched situation.

A final way signs supply a subjunctive vision is by pressing for *alternatives*. The effort begins with a strong iconic sign that has already been reflected back to a group. It is then taken a step further in a hypothetical move by asking: What if? When congregational imagination has become atrophied, this approach can provoke members to consider alternatives of their own invention. For instance, those who study congregations frequently use a timeline exercise as a reflective tool. Reviewing how the group has reached this moment in time can powerfully reveal its currently perceived history and values.[12] Participants are often surprised to see repeated patterns and behaviors that originated long before any of them were members but still make their influence felt today. To stop there would be frustrating, however. A final move in the process is then to ask: What should our next chapter be? What would happen if, in that chapter, we altered those practices or changed those structures that have dominated our history? Such a challenge takes seriously the signs of the context as it stands while giving space and permission for creatively rethinking what might happen next.

Using Signs in a Congregation

Let us extend the case study that has concluded the last two chapters in order to see how the pastor there shaped the raw insights gained through fieldwork tools into an interpretation of strong signs. Recall that his study began from a hunch about a lost sense of "appropriateness." The congregation seemed to have forgotten how to live as disciples or act as church. The pastor therefore wanted to learn how that situation was related to interpersonal relationships among members. This research problem offered a workable scope for his efforts, which he further refined by focusing on questions of power and values (political and symbolic frames) as well as home, family, and church (micro and meso frames). With this sort of framing, the pastor then used each of the four tools from the previous chapter during the course of his regular ministry, gradually assembling insights that began to hint at answers. Near the end of this work, he could see the paradox that his congregation was both sustained and endangered by its internal bonds.

It is worthwhile to remember at this point that the pastor's study was grounded in a larger care, respect, and hope for the congregation. He wanted to engage his listeners with a life-giving proclamation, a task that called in turn for a fresh and honest look at the setting. Divorced from these pastoral interests, the fieldwork results summarized near the end of chapter 3 might sound negative, whereas the pastor treated them as valuable clues to a complex and faithful people. In addition, these results emerged from a purposely narrowed research focus that did not try to examine everything about the congregation. The pastor was quite aware of other strong and promising aspects of the situation that would also be important for contextually attuned preaching. We cannot account for the all of this in the scope of these remarks. Instead, we will attend mainly to the pastor's interpretive conclusions. Using pithy, memorable phrases, he ultimately named four strong signs predominant in the congregation's life. Each drew from the use of several different tools. Each could be both a mirror of and window for the congregation. Most importantly, each was like a distinctive motif in a musical composition, at times in the foreground while at other times not, but together evoking an overall mood.

The first strong sign was called "Ties that bind." Through the years, the driving mission of the congregation became increasingly directed toward internal affiliations. Dense webs of interpersonal relations between members were now inviolable, having a virtually sacred quality. Perceived threats to these relations were answered by personalized attacks and incivility. Just as potent, when each person's life was so well known, information and secrets were used to enforce order. Even so, dissatisfaction with the level of constraint and coercion was growing. Many in the congregation were weary of this uneasy dance to which they were obliged. In addition, it was also clear that the very bonds between members could, at times, become channels for tremendous goodness and genuine care. Acts of prayer, words of concern, and deeds of charity were also part of these close ties, extending sometimes even to those beyond the congregation. Sadly, however, the bonds out of which openness and generosity could flow were marred by insecurity.

Another strong sign was called "Let it be." Due to close interpersonal relations, vast behavioral elbow room existed in the congregation. Each person's conduct was given wide berth. On the one hand, this showed a remarkable and gracious ability to let people be who they are, quirks and all, and to value something good about them even so. As a result, a forgiving or at least lenient disposition was the unspoken rule. On the other hand, though, this led to extremes and excesses. Some members, particularly those from deeply embedded and long-standing clans, could get away with almost anything. Hampered by a tendency to excuse or overlook this, the congregation could not challenge or confront such behavior and was therefore complicit in the problem. This sign spoke to the lack of appropriate boundaries the pastor had noticed from the start. Forgiveness had become twisted into tolerant endurance that actually contributed to harm, since nothing was ever truly unacceptable.

The third among these strong signs was called "Born to rule." Leadership positions were matters of inheritance rather than gifts or calling. This tightly bound congregation used prominent roles of authority to honor key people and reward proper compliance. While elected offices were subject to a typical rotation, the cadre of those who held them remained basically unchanged. For roles lacking selection or succession procedures, however, the same person might remain in power for decades. Aside from ignoring the abilities or talents of newcomers, this birthright system was a growing burden even for insiders who supported it. It was indeed refreshing that members were not disposable due to age or ableness. At the same time, however, the purpose of leadership changed from developing a vision to receiving a reward. Even those in authority felt unable to escape, let alone pass along the wisdom they had gained. A well-intentioned effort to show respect was undermining the congregation's resources and future.

The last of these strong signs was called the "Hell you know" motif (as in the saying, "The hell you know is better than the one you don't"). This congregation was in fact surprisingly candid about itself. It was keenly aware of many of its deepest problems. Members spoke freely and even bluntly about the situation, even to the point of laughing about their own foibles and flaws. Yet knowing these challenges was not the same as overcoming them. People were instead dismayed, not knowing what to do. Conversations about change ran into seemingly intractable barriers caused by close bonds and old patterns. Years of carefully maintained stasis had left members atrophied about how to imagine let alone implement even the smallest changes. They hoped for renewal and were truly eager for it to happen, but enthusiasm was dampened by what seemed to be their fate. Although resigned to who they had become and a little resentful about it, this was still better than attempting an alternative.

In a compact way, these four signs powerfully conveyed the deepest sense of what this pastor had learned. Far from being burdensome, they opened up motifs on which he could build. Beyond this, they became the basis for his further theological questions. What were the real sources of life and hope for the congregation? How could their penchant for survival be exposed as insecure if not idolatrous? What would be good news that might free them from webs of their own making? How could their bonds be loosened just a bit to risk care and concern for others? Most of all, what shape would preaching need to take in order to engage the strong signs of this place? We noted earlier that the four signs named by this pastor were like the motifs of a musical composition, together evoking an overall mood. The challenge for contextual preaching would now be to use these motifs in creating a new song.

Chapter 5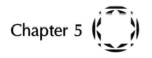

How Preaching Works with Context

In a famous cartoon drawn by Sidney Harris over thirty years ago, two scientists stand before a blackboard covered with equations. Interrupting the obscure symbols, however, are four simple words: "Then a miracle occurs . . ." Pointing to the phrase, the older scholar says to the younger, "I think you should be more explicit here in step two."[1] The joke comes uncomfortably close to what preaching books often seem to do. Having outlined all the relevant preparatory strategies, the actual move into the practice of preaching is left unsaid, as if it required a miracle. There are several understandable reasons for this silence. First, if proclamation still seeks a divine encounter, then even the most disciplined procedures for study and reflection include space for the Spirit's interruption and inspiration. This is no justification for lazy or sloppy preparation but instead shows a humble reliance on something more than our own wisdom. Second, we cannot specify in advance a uniform route toward proclamation because each preacher is distinctive. Any approach must be adjusted to a preacher's particular calling and gifts, and even then the process may change from one week to the next.

The matter seems only more complicated when it comes to contextual preaching. Of course, the purpose of this book has never been to provide a general overview of how to develop a sermon. Instead, the presupposition is that you either already have developed a responsible and reliable discipline for proclamation or are rapidly moving in this direction. There is no mistaking, however, that we have advocated for seriously addressing the situated nature of your preaching. The point has actually *not* been to add further steps to an existing process but rather to evoke a theological orientation to context, one informed by using frames, tools, and signs. Yet since this perspective may be unfamiliar, we also cannot avoid the question of when or how your renewed awareness of a context might intersect with sermon construction and presentation.

It is helpful to remember, as noted near the start of chapter 4, that your careful work of asking questions, gathering insights, and discerning signs in your local setting has already affected your preaching in significant ways. This new awareness has altered how you structure your ideas and select your words, even if you do not yet fully perceive the changes. Likewise, there is a new awareness of you as preacher, for your congregation sees the efforts you have taken to know them better, and this in turn affects how they listen. All of this is quite at odds with superficial views of contextual preaching that sprinkle local commentary into the sermon in order to illustrate, entertain, or manipulate. By contrast, you have begun to engage your listeners and their worlds in ways that honor the depth of what is happening there, especially its theological import. This is a truly integrated approach to contextual preaching. Now the question becomes, how can this become a regular and reliable practice?

Toward this end, let us return to the case study we have followed through the course of this book. The minister and congregation in that case surely differ greatly from you and your setting, but together you share a pastoral commitment to know your preaching context. The purpose of going one final step with this case study is certainly not to depict an ideal example to imitate. Instead, we simply wish to notice how a preacher not so different from yourself connected with his listeners through specific sermon devices and strategies in order to effect a potent theological engagement. Before turning to examples from sermons, we look first at how his preaching was part of the larger course of ministry in that congregation. Following the examples, we will then offer guidelines for how sound contextual preaching can be sustained over the long run, with attention to Scripture, sermons, and preachers.

Contextual Preaching and Other Ministries

It is pleasant to imagine that preaching empowered by contextual insights will provoke decisive changes in a congregation. This heroic fantasy rarely becomes reality, however, mainly because preaching is only one aspect of pastoral ministry and leadership, and sometimes may not be the most beneficial way to address a congregation's context. Effective pastors know that an ensemble effort is required that deploys many forms of ministry beyond the pulpit. This was certainly true for the pastor we met through the case study unfolded in the last three chapters. As we saw earlier, the members of his congregation could acknowledge their plight and even talk about it rather plainly. Indeed, they wanted the pastor to be a further catalyst for this and welcomed his help in exploring their situation with greater depth and honesty. Because his study of the context laid the groundwork for trust, this pastor felt he received a kind of permission to tell the truth about what he had discovered, even from the pulpit.

Even so, the pastor knew the massive challenges he had uncovered would call for various forms of truth telling that could work gradually and mutually. Different people in a range of venues would need to be included in the process. Actual changes would have to come in small, collaborative steps. These remarks are anything but off the subject of this chapter. Despite his serious interest in contextually attuned preaching, this pastor paradoxically began to recognize what his preaching *could not do* in relation to what he learned about his congregation. Although his central interest (and ours in his case) was with preaching, his first response to the strong signs of his context did not come from the pulpit. As he reflected on the results of his contextual study, it became clear that other forms of ministry offered better ways to begin addressing the situation, and would in turn set the scene for more deliberately contextual preaching yet to come.

The wisdom of the pastor's strategy is worth reviewing. For example, he soon began to review with congregational leaders on various committees and boards what his study had revealed. He invited their acknowledgment of the situation and explored their sense of whether matters should remain as they presently stood. By amplifying the contrasts within the context (using signs as a mirror) and then pressing alternatives to these (using signs as a window), the pastor was able to marshal consent and support of members to move in new directions. In addition, all parties agreed for the first time to mutual standards for acceptable behavior in congregational gatherings and communication, holding one another accountable in order to assure that the dignity of every member would henceforth be paramount.

What followed next were a series of modest changes. Trying to confront the tight bonds that paralyzed change and atrophied imagination would surely have evoked defensiveness and been fruitless. Instead, the pastor worked with many different members to introduce seemingly innocuous innovations. The piano was relocated within the worship space, which to everyone's surprise did lead to fighting or schism. Fellowship dinners were introduced to retrace the congregation's history, especially the challenges they had successfully weathered, with the events being widely attended and enjoyed. The purpose of these innovations was not change itself, but what they showed about no longer being trapped by conventional ways or accusatory reactions. A new vision was being opened. Indeed, the possibility for positive change became so real that an obstructive person on the paid staff was finally dismissed. Far from creating chaos, the firing was spoken of as a welcome relief and long overdue. Within another year, languishing efforts at building repair were transformed into a major capital campaign to make the facility available for community use. Members were shocked to realize what they had actually agreed to do but at the same time boasted at showing a boldness lacking in nearly two generations.

During this process of involving new leaders and introducing ever more complex changes, the pastor was firm about not staking his role on getting his own way. With subtlety, patience, good partners, and a healthy sense of his own limits, he helped the congregation see a new horizon for itself, one that did not rely on old patterns of dependency and control. More significant than even this, the pastor kept in the foreground that he had been called to be a *pastor*. Ordinary forms of pastoral ministry like visiting the sick, counseling and consolation, teaching Scripture, prayer and devotions, and worship leadership were not neglected. As it turned out, this pastor's contextual study actually affected these other kinds of ministry as profoundly as anything he would eventually preach.

It was in this milieu of honesty, partnership, change, and ministry that the pastor's preaching became more contextually engaged. As we have just seen, however, preaching was not the first or even the central way of addressing the situation but simply one alongside others. The pastor ventured that, at least initially, his preaching would be most faithful with the situation by offering a steady word of assurance and hope, interpreting for the congregation how the changes and challenges before them were part of a larger story of God's promise. In other words, he sought a rather ordinary and low-profile way for preaching to address his listeners and their worlds. Perhaps contrary to our expectations, he did not develop a special sermon series with a strong contextual focus, simply because the issues at stake in the congregation were so pervasive and ongoing. Nor did he intentionally foreground certain contextual themes or topics as a new preaching agenda, on the suspicion that these would soon sound tiresome and obvious.

Upon reflection, this pastor acknowledged that his "plan" for contextual preaching simply came down to listening closely for the many surprising ways that the strong signs in the local setting resonated with the Scriptures selected for preaching, and thus suggested an alternative theological vision for the congregation. He was ever on the lookout for how his listeners might glimpse their ordinary context as part of a larger world that God was transforming. Using indirection, subtlety, images, and even humor, he tried to open up a view of new life in Christ that he feared had been forgotten. This preacher repeatedly showed that contextual preaching was not a matter of style or technique but of persistent theological awareness of what is at stake for a local setting in an encounter with Scripture through preaching. Since this steady effort was rooted in the strong signs of the congregation, it was inevitable that his preaching would thereby address the most significant challenges they faced and what the hope in these might be.

A Study of Contextual Preaching

We turn now to review this pastor's contextual preaching, using both a main example and portions taken from a few other sermons. The special value of these examples is that they are *not* flawless models or ideal types. They are instead specific instances of this pastor's regular Sunday preaching as actually presented in the congregation. From your own point of view, you may find in them problematic moves or missed opportunities, but these are also instructive. Our aim was simply to show ordinary proclamation, as fine and as flawed as any of your own. To be sure, it would have been interesting to choose from many such sermons at random and then look for indications of contextual engagement or detachment. The scope of this book required, however, that we select a few brief, compelling examples. You should also know that these sermons were preached more than a year after the pastor's fieldwork ended, and all but one within a two-month period. They are not fresh on the heels of recent research and flush with enthusiasm. Instead, they result from a longer, patient process of reflection in which the preacher let his initial insights about the context settle in deeply.

The main example that follows is based on Matthew 3:13-17, recounting Jesus' baptism by John in the Jordan, and was preached on the festival of the Baptism of Jesus. Paragraphs from the sermon manuscript are numbered sequentially for ease of reference in the commentary that follows. Portions of other sermons are incorporated into that commentary as appropriate:

1. Worse than acne. Worse than book reports. Worse than slipping on the ice in front of the cutest kid in the class. What is the worst experience in a kid's life? Dancing in gym class. I shudder just to think of it. It really is inhumane, a cruel and unusual punishment. What gym teacher in his or her right mind would expect grade school boys and girls to hold hands in public, to pull each other close, to make what is about the most awkward time in life even worse? But still they do it . . . always have, always will. Perhaps gym teachers take some perverse pleasure in watching adolescents squirm. Or maybe it's payback for their own horrendous memories of waltzing torture under some sadistic gym teacher from the past.

2. "Class, find a partner," the teacher barks. "Gentlemen, take her right hand in your left. Yes, *that* right hand. Will this kill you? No, but *I* might. Now, with your left foot, take one step forward and . . ." Whatever instructions follow are soon lost in the fog of adolescent shame. Boy-girl partners? Holding hands? Every kid in the room is thinking, "Just shoot me. Let me drop through the floor. Anything but this." Of course, the outcome isn't all that bad. Most often, the reluctant students simply close their eyes, take a deep breath, and stumble over each other's feet for the next thirty minutes, dying a slow, agonizing death with each misplaced step.

3. That scene has been repeated a hundred times before. It happened again just this last week at my daughter's school. This time, though, there was a bit of a twist, and she told me I could tell you about it. Just when the dance instructions began, one of the guys in the class decided he had had enough. "No," he muttered through clenched teeth, his resentment a thin veil for his shame. "What?" the teacher snapped back. The boy crossed his arms across his chest, planted his feet on the floor, and glared right back at the teacher. "No. I won't dance." You've got to give the kid points for guts . . . but not for smarts. He learned that day that the gym teacher always wins. He simply wasn't about to humiliate himself in front of his classmates. "No. I won't dance." God bless him. Perhaps one day we can visit him in prison.

4. It's not only grade school children who are reluctant to enter the dance. As we get older, we learn how to refuse without being so blunt about it. We pretend not to hear. We lose the memo. We drag our feet. We call in sick. We all learn how to do this. Everyone, that is, but John the Baptizer.

5. "Baptize me," Jesus said.
    "What?" John replied. "No. I won't baptize you."
    "Baptize me."
    "No. I won't. It's not right."
    "Baptize me. You have to. It's the next step in the dance."

6. Like that obstinate boy in my daughter's grade school, John the Baptizer wasn't about to take Jesus' hand and waltz down to the river with him. It wasn't that John was embarrassed. A man who wears camel-hair tunics and eats bugs doesn't embarrass easily. John knew it simply wasn't his place. He had been waiting to kneel before Jesus, not to have Jesus bow before him.

7. Matthew is the only one of the Gospel writers to pull John and Jesus out of the water and shove them on the dance floor for a lesson. When John the Baptizer balked at baptizing Jesus, our Lord had an answer. You heard it earlier in all of its formality. Jesus told John, "Let it be so now, for it is proper for us in this way to fulfill all righteousness." You see, up to this point, John had been willing to do many things. He was willing to repent and tell others

to do the same. He was willing to alienate his hearers, calling them a brood of vipers, and then call them to live more justly. But now, Jesus needed John to do the one thing for which he wasn't quite ready. Jesus needed John to enter into righteousness.

8. Righteousness was what Jesus came to bring, to fulfill. It meant to live out completely the purposes of God. It meant to do the will of God, reflect the image of God, bear the promise of God. The righteousness Jesus brings, the righteousness he demands of John that day at the river, was a life of submission. It was to hand over his life instead of to grasp and take. It was to follow God's way, not to lead. And Jesus insisted that John be part of this kind of righteousness, the righteousness that would be fulfilled on the cross. "Take my hand," Jesus said to John. "You can do this."

9. Scholars have debated for centuries why it was that Jesus, the sinless Son of God, had to be baptized in the first place. I wonder today, reading it again, if the baptism wasn't so much for Jesus' sake as it was for John's. Maybe, like a grade school gym teacher, Jesus knew that the next step for John was going to be a hard one. John knew how to preach, how to draw a crowd, how to lead with power. Did he know how to follow? It was time for John to submit to someone else's lead, to let someone else call the steps, to place his hand in Jesus' and stumble along.

10. This whole following someone else's lead thing isn't easy for anyone. When we feel confident about the next step, we wouldn't dream of letting someone else call the tune. We don't need a partner then. And if we are frightened or feeling off balance, the last thing we want to do is let someone drag us out onto the dance floor where we are sure to make fools of ourselves, sure to fall. It's true for us as individuals, it's true for families, and it's especially true for congregations. Even ours.

11. In the last few months, God has dragged our little church out onto the floor countless times. And each time, to our astonishment, we have learned the steps. For the first time in years, we are getting along: forgiving each other when we mess up, holding each other's hands over the rough spots, laughing off things that used to end in a brawl. No one really expected that we could find money for a new building project, but God taught us a thing or two. We not only met our goal but exceeded it by a third. You would think that with all this newfound confidence, having mastered a set of complicated and delicate steps, we would be able to say, "Okay, Jesus, let's dance some more. What's next?"

12. Instead, we are inching back toward the wall. Money will be tight in the coming year. (When isn't it?) Bigger decisions than we've already made loom before us. The potential for disagreement and second-guessing is enormous,

and we have more than our share of armchair quarterbacks. On top of all that, business is squishy, schools are a mess, work is uncertain, war rages on. There are plenty of reasons for our knees to knock and our palms to sweat.

13.   As hesitant as an eleven-year-old boy is to dance, as reluctant as John was to baptize his master, so cautious are we. We worry and wonder about taking the next step, whether it's a whole congregation edging toward the door, or one person saying, "No, thanks, I'll sit this one out." We worry and wonder because we think that we must be in charge, that the responsibility is entirely ours, as well as the blame. But Jesus asks us, baptized just like him, to enter into his righteousness. He invites us to submit. He beckons us to hand ourselves over. He calls us to follow, with him in the lead.

14.   It's really not that hard. The dance into which Jesus invites us is not too difficult for us. He is relentless in pursuing us as partners—not impatient or harsh, but persistent and encouraging. He will not ask us to do what we cannot, though he will surely ask before we are ready. And once we step out onto the floor, his leading is secure. To John he once said, "Baptize me. It's the right thing to do." To us he says, "Dance with me. I'll show you how."

One reason this particular sermon was chosen as the main example for this chapter is the listener response it elicited. Days and weeks later, members spoke of how they saw themselves in the sermon, using remarks like "You really nailed it!" and "How did you know?" At the same time, it is apparent that this was no heavy-handed, brow-beating sermon. The preacher took a deft approach toward a difficult contextual reality not directly named until ¶12. Obviously, there are other ways to preach based on this same biblical text. For example, another sermon might have focused on the nature of baptism itself in relation to Jesus' baptism. In this case, however, the pastor wanted for contextual reasons to have listeners identify more closely with the figure of John and his initial refusal. Thinking back to the end of chapter 4 and the four strong signs that this pastor memorably labeled, we can see that his main focus here was on the "Hell you know" sign. Wearily resigned to its circumstances, this congregation preferred its present fate to any alternatives. In broad strokes, the sermon deployed that sign as both mirror and window. As a mirror of what already is, it was used to reacquaint the congregation in ¶11 to how far they had come, offering a new appreciation for what may have grown stale. As a window of what might yet be, the sign was used for reconnection, conveying in ¶¶12–13 that the congregation was part of Jesus' mission of righteousness. Of course, this is simply to indicate the ends toward which the sermon strove. The detailed challenge now is to show what led to this throughout the sermon, especially several distinctive strategies found in sound contextual preaching.

Realizing that he wanted to approach a difficult contextual issue that might provoke defensiveness, the preacher adopted a strategy of *indirection*. From the very start, he unfolded a simple, familiar, even homely story from childhood, one that was immediately accessible to all. This was no attempt to begin with an entertaining, lighthearted anecdote. The issue was far more serious. The preacher wanted to create a rich narrative world in ¶¶1–2 that would dislodge his listeners from their present situation. As the beginning of ¶3 hinted, the story aimed at images and feelings remarkably widespread among those raised in the United States, even across age and class lines. Moreover, the narrative further pulled listeners in an unexpected direction by introducing a wrinkle in ¶3. By this point, the congregation had left its conventional worlds behind, which allowed the preacher to return to that reality in surprising ways later.

The indirection did not end there, however. The sudden turn to the biblical story near the end of ¶4 supplied a new layer. Listeners would naturally assume that the sermon was making a basic analogy about "resistance" that linked the opening story from gym class to the scene at the Jordan River. While that was somewhat true, it was certainly not the whole story. In any case, the imaginary conversation in ¶5 offered a new and vivid scene, created here through a present-tense dialogue. The subsequent development and probing of that story in ¶¶6–9 only situated listeners ever deeper in concerns seemingly remote from their own. Consider how much of the sermon has transpired by now (over half of its overall content) and how far from its own context the congregation had been transported. Despite the passing gesture to listeners' lives during ¶4, the sermon's real impact for the local setting was not finally disclosed until ¶10. Even then, there were several more turns until the troubling focus of the sermon was reached. The point for us is that contextual preaching sometimes calls upon indirection (creating alternative worlds, withholding key connections, or deferring local impact) in order to prepare people to hear what they otherwise might dismiss about their situation. A little bit of distance can go a long way toward bringing listeners willingly back home.

The strategy of indirection was also noticeable in another of this pastor's sermons preached just a few weeks later. Based on Matthew 4:12-23, only the opening paragraphs of that sermon are reproduced here. At first glance, this selection again shows little immediate connection with the congregational context:

Simon and Andrew, James and John had long ago given up dreaming of importance or notice. They were born to be fishermen. They didn't need a high school guidance counselor to help them select a career path. In fact, they hadn't gone to high school, couldn't read or write. You didn't need a formal education to do what they did. Get up early. Work like a dog. Clean like a slave. Sleep like the dead. Repeat the next day for about fifty years. No one envied what they did, no one cared what they thought. They were just fishermen, like their fathers, like their sons. You can imagine their surprise when Jesus called out to them on the docks. At first they figured he was a tourist wanting to know the price of the day's catch. That's all anyone ever asked them. But Jesus wasn't buying fish that day. He was calling fishermen. Calling them to fish waters they'd never sailed before, waters they'd never really *wanted* to sail before.

In my current stack of reading is a new book about leadership. While waiting at the dentist's office the other day, I read this: "We have come to believe that safety is the most important value in life. But if a society is to evolve, then safety can never be allowed to become more important than adventure. Everything we enjoy as part of our advanced civilization came about because previous generations made adventure more important that safety."[2] Some are called to political office. Some are called to ministry. Some are called to fish. None of us are called to safety.

The thing that mystifies me about this story from Matthew is that, at the sound of Jesus' voice, Simon and Andrew, James and John dropped their nets and raced after him. They didn't know who he was, where he was going, what they would be doing. Their family had fished for generations. It was all they knew. Maybe they were reading my leadership book. Maybe they were tired of fishing. Or maybe that same Spirit that lighted on Jesus at the River Jordan landed on their heads as well, whispering in their ears that it was time to get off their wet rear ends, drop their bulky nets, and follow. We have no way to know. How many others did Jesus call that day? How many heard his voice and ignored it? How many wouldn't even remember seeing Jesus? But a few heard. A few looked up. A few followed. And those few changed the world.

Note that several new forms of indirection were involved. The sermon immediately plunged the listener into a narrative world, but this time the biblical story. Entering that world on its own terms virtually required disconnecting from one's own situation. At the same time, that world was not totally foreign. The words resonated deeply with contemporary listeners in terms of daily and even generational patterns of labor, insignificance, and futility. A further indirection came with the preacher's sudden mention of a book on leadership. Though a contemporary text, it was unrelated to the disciples and perhaps just as distant from listeners. An almost distracting little puzzle was introduced: Where is this going? The return to the disciples in the final part of this selection finally forged the deeper point: Jesus' call creates risk and promises new life. Since you already know some of the background of this context, it is not hard to imagine how the sermon then turned directly toward the present challenges facing this congregation. In order for listeners to make that turn, however, required an extended period of indirection.

Let us return to the main sermon example to look at other strategies employed by this preacher. We said in chapter 4 that contextual preaching uses strong signs in an overall concern for telling the truth. This same concern was evident in the main sermon through various strategies of *acknowledgment*. The objective of these strategies was for listeners to hear and accept an otherwise discomforting aspect of the biblical text or local situation. For example, the preacher frequently used humor in this fashion, not to amuse but to generate a "Yes, it's really that way" reaction. The exaggerated remark about prison at the end of ¶3 actually underscored that resistance can be costly, which led into the supposedly mature forms of refusal in ¶4 that most people have used. The offbeat comment about John's clothing and diet in ¶6 actually refocused listeners to learn what was at stake when he refused Jesus' request. Even the amusing tone of the gym-class story actually became a way for listeners to reclaim through levity something that might instead cause them to wince. In a related way, humor can contribute to the strategy of acknowledgment by defusing tension at a more serious point in the sermon, as with the extreme physical reactions mentioned at the end of the rather sober ¶12.

Other kinds of acknowledgment happened through what could be called "leading." For instance, the shift in ¶4 from grade school to adult forms of resistance was a way of leading from easier or safer cases to harder ones, thus creating new acknowledgment. A similar approach came in the move from individual to congregational life at the end of ¶10. Another form of leading happened with remarks that blurred the line between biblical and contemporary worlds. In this sermon and others, the preacher helped his listeners find themselves within a scriptural scene by inserting contemporary references into the retelling of ancient texts, as with the use of modern-dance motifs in ¶6 and ¶9. A different kind of leading can be found through the general affective valence of the sermon, which lent a deeper existential significance to the sermon. The physical and emotional clumsiness at the end of ¶2 provoked profound memories of humiliation and shame, while the struggle to retain confident composure in ¶10 suggested the insecurity and fear that often drives human action. One last type of leading was conveyed through the compassionate tone of the sermon, which led into breaking the silence about topics previously taboo for this congregation. The simple, appreciative vision offered in ¶11 gave the preacher a basis for moving into a harder set of truths in ¶¶12–13.

A few other aspects of this strategy of acknowledgment can be detected in another of this preacher's sermons. Based on John 1:29-42, it was preached the very next week after the main sermon example above. The selected portion came near the end of the sermon, just after the preacher recounted how the disciples of John the Baptist began to follow after Jesus:

Jesus' first words to them were, "What are you looking for?" Words suddenly failed them. They could have told him about John's description of the baptism. They could have told him about their life-long quest for the Messiah. They could have asked if they could follow. Instead they blurted out the stupidest thing they could: "Uh . . . where are you staying?" Tongue-tied in Jesus' presence. Instead of directing them to MapQuest or describing the place he was living, he gave them little information but a full answer: "Come and see." Come and see. What more did he really need to say? There was both too much to tell them on that noisy street corner and nothing else that mattered. Come and see: the first, the best, the only invitation to discipleship.

Today we hold our annual meeting. For most pastors I know, it is the most dreaded of church festivals, driving some to drink, others to despair. In some congregations, these meetings can be pure torture. I've seen treasurers reduced to tears, committee chairs cornered like frightened rabbits, congregation presidents reduced to mush. "Why didn't you? Why did you? Who decided this? Who's going to pay for that?" Christians are often not on best behavior at such times. When otherwise reasonable people go on the attack, implying mismanagement or incompetence or conspiracy or worse, I have to wonder, "What are you looking for?" It is probably easier for those unfamiliar with the faith, those who have never met Jesus to answer that question. But for those who have been part of congregations all their lives, it is a harder nut to crack. If annual meetings are any indication, it appears we are looking for control and certainty and sameness. Is that what Jesus calls us to see? The same thing we saw yesterday?

If would-be disciples were asked, "What are you looking for?" most would not answer contentious church meetings or lengthy reports or *Roberts Rules of Order* or a diatribe on the way we've always done things. I know what seekers are looking for. It's really what we all are looking for. Disciples are looking for a teacher. Orphans long for home. The hungry seek a meal. Sinners beg forgiveness. Mourners pray comfort. The young itch for a challenge. Victims crave safety. Dare we invite them to come and see? Will they find here any of the things they so desperately desire? Will they see Jesus?

It comes as no surprise that several devices used in this portion were similar to the strategies of acknowledgment discussed earlier. The blurring between present and past occurred several times during the textual treatment at the outset, while the affective valence of group conflicts and human hopes was evident in the remaining moves. Even so, there were important differences in how contextual acknowledgment happened in this sermon selection. While the main focus seemed to be on the congregation's own meetings, most of that description actually concerned *other* pastors and churches, introducing "we" only quite near the end of those remarks. This sidestepping allowed listeners to ponder whether they had ever acted similarly. Certain unsavory aspects of their recent past could thereby be named and claimed. Against that backdrop, moreover, listeners could then begin to identify with the deeper longings mentioned in the final part. The sharp contrast between annual meetings and lasting hopes thereby let listeners reclaim who they really wished to be, as well as what that might mean for ministry toward others.

One last time, we return to the main sermon example to consider a final strategy used by this preacher. For the sake of engaging the preaching context in this sermon, he relied especially on core metaphors for *rethinking*. As noted earlier, one of the several features that contributes to a strong sign is its inclusion of both sides of a tension or paradox. Only in this way can such a sign convey an appropriately honest and complex sense of reality. The main sermon showed this by using the dominant image of dance throughout its overall flow. We have already seen how dance was called upon at major points to speak not only about fear and humiliation in ¶¶2–3 and ¶10, but also daring and aspiration in ¶11. In numerous smaller ways, however, the image provided a sort of connective tissue throughout the whole, with dance-related terms deployed at nearly every step along the way. Of particular importance in this sermon was the way dance as a metaphor opened up a new understanding in ¶7 about what it meant for John and Jesus to "fulfill all righteousness." By the end of ¶9, the image allowed the preacher to link that righteousness to a cruciform disposition, submitting to God's ways even unto death, with Jesus in the lead. The rethinking enabled through a dominant image is quite important for contextually attuned preaching. Without such an accessible strategy for connections, the biblical text can remain opaque and distant from the preaching context it intends to affect.

Not only was the Scripture considered anew through this core metaphor but also the identity and purpose of the congregation itself. One of the implicit dimensions of this sermon and the day on which it was preached, which only briefly becomes explicit in ¶13, is that the baptism of Jesus relates somehow to the baptism of every Christian. By using the image of dance in relation to John and Jesus in the text, contemporary listeners were invited to reflect on their own baptismal identity in the same terms. Interestingly, that new picture of baptism was in kinesic rather than cognitive terms. Baptism was therefore not so much about ideas or beliefs as it concerned how the listeners might act, as mentioned in ¶8, and the next steps they could take, as stated in ¶¶13–14. Moreover, since dance in this case was presented as a social interaction, it helped listeners to see beyond the isolated and individualistic quality of faith that so captivated this congregation. In the end, the use of dance offered a new story line for them, one not driven by familiar bonds but by a risky venture in the embrace of God.

For a quite different example of a strategy of rethinking, we turn to a sermon from half year earlier. Based on Luke 12:49-56, the sermon focused especially on the verses about household division. After initial remarks about typical family annoyances, the following selection then comprised the middle of the sermon:

Those of us from less-than-perfect families perk up our ears when Jesus talks about divided families. How does he know? His blunt words seem frighteningly accurate. Far from being unique, we find that family squabbles and hatreds are ancient. But before we use Jesus' words to justify skipping the next family gathering, we need to think about where Jesus is. He is not on vacation. He is marching, marching himself toward death. Knowing that before long everyone you love will run for cover and you'll hang on a cross puts things in perspective. Jesus has lost his sense of humor. His followers slip into the shadows. His enemies creep out of the woodwork. Soon he will be hard-pressed to find anyone to trust, family or friend. And the Timid Twelve either don't get it or don't want to. It's going to get worse, Jesus says. Your fathers will turn on you, your mothers will pretend you were never born, your in-laws will take your photo off the mantel, and your children will say you are dead. Because you know me, no one will want to know you.

Truth is, Jesus' honest words about families are not about our families at all. Most of us don't get along in our families because someone is stubborn or selfish, holding a grudge or nursing a wound. Of course, we would never do anything like that. It's them, our ungrateful, petty, practically criminal relatives who make family life so hard. No, we are wonderful people, forgiving, open-minded, generous. Who wouldn't want to be related to us? But the divisions of which Jesus speaks have nothing to do with your aunt's smelly dog, your cousin's drinking problem, the feud over Grandma's estate, or your mother's addiction to daytime television. With few exceptions, our family troubles stem from cold hearts and long memories. Those petty hurts and decades-old feuds count for nothing to Jesus at this point. If we are to be his disciples, they would mean nothing to us either.

Can you imagine if our families were divided because we chose to follow Jesus? Then the story would be different. If we fought over how best to be faithful, Jesus might just step in. If we bickered about how much to give to the poor, half our wealth or all of it, we might get his attention. Don't get me wrong. I don't think Jesus is unsympathetic to family sorrows. But there are times when our needs are not the most pressing thing in the world, when our sorrows should take a back seat to the sorrows of the whole human family, all of God's children. Jesus marches toward his death, keenly aware of his dying relatives: soldiers and civilians at war, children with empty stomachs, addicts trapped in despair, the sick and elderly with no future but the grave. When our concerns are for *that* family, yes, others might reject us. When we stand firmly on the side of peace, forgiveness, and mercy, some will write us off. But then we find another family, the family of the faithful, committed to Jesus' way rather than our own.

It is not hard to sense the pastor's initial hunch and research problem coming through in this sermon. After all, his congregation was afflicted by its own tight bonds. These were typically expressed in family metaphors that were both unblemished and unassailable. Yet the pastor knew from his research that these "Ties that bind" were more troubling and frayed than appearances suggested. It was necessary not simply to introduce realism into the situation but especially to offer a way for rethinking what family in the household of faith might truly mean. Therefore, words of apparent sympathy for our fractured families at the opening of this selection were then undercut by recalling that Jesus said them not in our comfortable homes but on his way to the cross. In that light, family began to look very different. More poignant still, by the end of this section listeners were able to consider a different vision for what family might mean, far broader than the local affiliations to which they were regularly accustomed.

Guidelines for Contextual Preaching Practice

Throughout this book, you have been introduced to a way of studying your context for the sake of more grounded preaching. Along the way, we traced the example of a pastor who followed this process, which in turn affected his preaching. That case study was not meant as the only or best way to do contextual preaching, but simply let us closely review how one preacher did so in relation to a few sermons and his own research. Your path will obviously look quite different. At this point, however, let us step back from any particular contextual study and ask a broader question: What are the general guidelines for a faithful and sustained practice of effective contextual preaching? Six broad guidelines come to the foreground.

First, *Scripture should be studied with local listeners.* As part of the larger stream of Christian proclamation, contextual preaching attends to the authoritative warrant of the biblical canon. That warrant was received through social pathways of the church and is treasured still in social gatherings of the church. To study Scripture for preaching in isolation from such social forms not only decontextualizes it from its natural home but also impedes your awareness of its actual impact for your listeners. Some portion of your regular preaching preparation should therefore involve your listeners in examining with you the biblical basis for the coming sermon.[3] This is exactly what the pastor in our case study did with two different study groups every week. At a basic level, it prepares your listeners to hear the sermon more fully. Far more than this, it allows you to learn their unaided responses and reactions to biblical texts. In this way, you can sense in advance both the confusing aspects that will require clarification and the deeper connections upon which you can build.

Second, *Scripture should be interpreted for its signs.* We discussed at length the strong signs that make sense of what is happening in a context. A similar approach can be used when looking at biblical texts for preaching. Of course, this presumes a responsible approach to Scripture study that would not reduce the particularity of texts down to themes or slogans for preaching. Yet sound exegetical process can still allow us to ask about the strong signs of a given text in a way that is comparable to discerning such signs in a particular context.[4] In the end, we seek to interact with the concrete plight and hopes of our ancestors in the faith. The God on whom they relied is also our God, and so their testimony and wisdom matters to us. That wisdom is often conveyed through existential meanings, paradoxical forms, and direct address, strong signs that point to the God in whom we all have placed our hope. Interaction between this sign language of Scripture and that of the local setting can give contemporary listeners a richer vocabulary for seeing their own lives, paired with a wider imagination for God's ongoing work.

Third, *sermons should be integrated with worship.* There is a natural tendency to think of the sermon as a self-contained entity, like an isolated work of art on a museum wall. Yet preaching has its own typical and dynamic context, that of the weekly assembly. We need to develop the habit of a contextualized view of contextual preaching, set amidst those gathered for worship.[5] Tremendous benefits accrue when the sermon is closely integrated with that setting. Rather than bearing all the weight for engaging the context, it can relate to and rely upon other forms of communal participation deployed in the gathering. Strong contextual preaching knows how to connect with songs of lament or praise, words of petition or blessing, and times of movement, silence, washing, or feeding. We noted earlier that contextually attuned preachers must first come to terms with what their preaching *cannot* do. In that light, attention to the worship setting allows us to call upon other forms beyond preaching that can also engage the context and, in turn, realize better what the sermon at a given moment *can* distinctively achieve.

Fourth, *sermons should aim at participatory encounter.* There are many fraudulent forms of contextual preaching. One of the most dreary is driven by information, offering a religious documentary on current events, perhaps enlightening but never compelling. Little better is that driven by moralizing, where the setting becomes fodder for advice and guidance, easily deflected if not dismissed. By contrast, sound contextual preaching is marked by being eventful. This does not mean that every such sermon leads to profound transformation of listeners. Instead, the sermon simply acts as if something of gravity were at stake, an encounter with the divine that might truly promise life. Such preaching unfolds in dynamic, concrete, sensory, and affective ways. It fundamentally tries to move its listeners somewhere, past their defenses against hearing the truth and beyond their myopia obscuring what God might have in mind for them. Its language and design aim to draw people into a new place of recognition and renewal.[6] Therefore, contextual preaching is deeply concerned about how its aesthetic relates to its situation.

Fifth, *preachers should evaluate sermons cumulatively.* With so much at stake in our preaching, it is easy to become discouraged at a lack of response to any one sermon. The context in which preaching has its impact is not just a given hour, day, or even week, however, but the ebb and flow of the faithful community in its broader time and place. Moving people to deeper honesty is not a short-term proposition. Therefore, preachers need a patient approach to assessing their work. Only after many months ought you review a moderate number of sermons to notice patterns across the whole. You may discover local concerns that you persistently engaged from many different angles. You may also be surprised by the gaps and undernourished aspects of your sermons that call for attention. Like the Scripture study mentioned earlier, this entire process of assessment should also involve local listeners. In their company, you can track the larger and longer conversation of which your preaching has been just a part, looking for how they have responded to or resisted your efforts.

Finally, *preachers should begin locally toward a wider horizon.* It is certainly fair at this point to wonder about the broader social focus of contextual preaching. As you know, most of our discussion herein has looked at the preaching context rather locally. This should not be mistaken for advocating parochialism. It is instead a question of the starting point. We focus on where people actually are, the ambit of life to which they regularly relate. A full exploration of any setting can never remain isolated, however, for it is automatically embedded in larger webs of significance and related to wide social and cultural ecologies. Rather than starting globally, which quickly becomes remote, overwhelming, and benumbing for listeners, we begin at home and then draw the wider implications. Indeed, what motivated the pastor in our case study was the hunch that until he addressed his local setting, they would never be able to move beyond themselves in ministry. In this respect contextual preaching follows an outward course familiar to the faithful of another era, when the first disciples were compelled by Jesus to "be my witnesses in Jerusalem, in all Judea and Samaria, and to the ends of the earth" (Acts 1:8). The path of all discipleship is centrifugal.[7] No less is true for the practice of contextual preaching.

Notes

Chapter 1 • How Context Matters in Preaching

1. For critique of such "technical rationality," see Donald A. Schön, *The Reflective Practitioner: How Professionals Think in Action* (New York: Basic, 1983), 21–49.

2. James R. Nieman, "What Is Preaching?" in *What Is Changing in Eucharistic Practice? Open Questions in Worship*, ed. Gordon Lathrop, vol. 5 (Minneapolis: Augsburg Fortress, 1995), 6–13.

3. Because "The speech of God is and remains the mystery of God supremely in its secularity," and "The secularity proper to God's Word is not in itself and as such transparent or capable of being the translucent garment or mirror of God's Word," therefore "The real interpretation of its form can only be that which God's word gives itself." Karl Barth, *Church Dogmatics*, vol. I/1, *The Doctrine of the Word of God*, ed. G. W. Bromiley and T. F. Torrance (Edinburgh: T&T Clark, 1975), 165–67; cf. 88–99, esp. 92–95.

4. Hannah Arendt, *Eichmann in Jerusalem: A Report on the Banality of Evil*, rev. ed. (New York: Penguin, 1977), 49.

5. Victoria J. Barnett, Wayne Whitson Floyd, Jr., and Barbara Wojhoski, eds., *Dietrich Bonhoeffer Works*, vol. 16, *Conspiracy and Imprisonment: 1940-1945*, ed. Mark S. Brocker, trans. Lisa E. Dahill (Minneapolis: Fortress Press, 2006), 605.

6. Such truth telling exhibits the theology of the cross, as expressed in Thesis 21 of Luther's 1518 Heidelberg Disputation: "A theology of glory calls evil good and good evil. A theology of the cross calls the thing what it actually is." Jaroslav Pelikan and Helmut T. Lehmann, eds., *Luther's Works*, vol. 31, *Career of the Reformer I*, ed. Harold J. Grimm (Philadelphia: Muhlenberg, 1957), 53.

7. James R. Nieman, "Why the Idea of Practice Matters," in *Teaching Preaching as a Christian Practice: A New Approach to Homiletical Pedagogy*, ed. Thomas G. Long and Nora Tubbs Tisdale (Louisville: Westminster John Knox, 2008), 18–40.

8. John Dominic Crossan, *The Dark Interval: Towards a Theology of Story* (Niles, Ill.: Argus Communications, 1975), 51–57. Crossan noted that narratives exist along a continuum running from the mythic, which mediates irreducible opposites in order to resolve tensions and evoke stability, to the parabolic, which challenges and disrupts any complacency by naming unforeseen and even disturbing possibilities. By being thoroughly situated, grounded preaching can implement both of these narrative options.

9. The phrase originates with: David H. Kelsey, *The Uses of Scripture in Recent Theology* (Philadelphia: Fortress Press, 1975), 172. It was first connected with contextual approaches to preaching in Leonora Tubbs Tisdale, *Preaching as Local Theology and Folk Art* (Minneapolis: Fortress Press, 1997), 43.

10. James R. Nieman and Thomas G. Rogers, *Preaching to Every Pew: Cross-Cultural Strategies* (Minneapolis: Fortress Press, 2001), 15.

11. St. Augustine, *On Christian Teaching*, trans. R. P. H. Green (New York: Oxford University Press, 1997), 117–19 [Book Four, XII.27-28]. The entire discussion of the aims of speaking and the duties of speaker is found in Book Four, XII.27–XV.32.

12. Ibid., 137 [Book Four, XXII.51]. The entire discussion of the three kinds of styles found in Book Four, XVI.33–XXVI.58.

13. Johannes Quasten and Joseph C. Plumpe, eds., *Ancient Christian Writers: The Works of the Fathers in Translation*, no. 11, St. Gregory the Great, *Pastoral Care (Regula Pastoralis)*, trans. Henry Davis (New York: Newman, 1950), 90 [Part Three, Prologue].

14. Guibert of Nogent, "How to Make a Sermon," in *The Library of Christian Classics*, ed. John Baillie, John T. McNeill, and Henry P. van Dusen, vol. 9, *Early Medieval Theology*, ed. and trans. George E. McCracken and Allen Cabaniss (Philadelphia: Westminster, 1957), 290.

15. Henry H. Mitchell, *Black Preaching: The Recovery of a Powerful Art* (Nashville: Abingdon, 1990), 105.

16. Improved communication and travel allow for rapid impact of even the most remote information and events, speeding the cycle of action and reaction that produces feelings of stress.

17. Widespread trade and migration bring ordinary people into regular and repeated contact with other cultures, views, and products. The term *glocalization* expresses this simultaneous influence of universal and particular tendencies. Roland Robertson, "Glocalization: Time-space and Homogeneity-heterogeneity," in *Global Modernities*, ed. Mike Featherstone, Scott Lash, and Roland Robertson (Thousand Oaks, Calif.: SAGE, 1995), 25–42.

18. The Second Vatican Council was a major catalyst for this by affirming the particular or local church in the Dogmatic Constitution on the Church, as well as the Decree on the Church's Missionary Activity. Austin Flannery, ed., *Vatican Council II*, vol. 1, *The Conciliar and Post Conciliar Documents*, rev. ed. (Northport, N.Y.: Castello, 1975), 376–78, 381–82 [*Lumen Gentium* III.23, 26], 835–40 [*Ad Gentes Divinitus* III.19-22].

19. This has been particularly apparent in how liberation theologies and practical theology attend to contexts. Early examples of this include: Edward Farley, "Interpreting Situations: An Inquiry into the Nature of Practical Theology," in *Formation and Reflection: The Promise of Practical Theology*, ed. Lewis S. Mudge and James N. Poling (Philadelphia: Fortress Press, 1987), 1–26; Robert J. Schreiter, *Constructing Local Theologies* (Maryknoll, N.Y.: Orbis, 1985).

20. The literature derived from or influenced by the "New Homiletic" is immense. Early examples include: David James Randolph, *The Renewal of Preaching: A New Homiletic Based on the New Hermeneutic* (Philadelphia: Fortress Press, 1969); Fred B. Craddock, *As One Without Authority* (Nashville: Abingdon, 1971). Collaborative implications of this were later explored in: John S. McClure, *The Roundtable Pulpit: Where Leadership and Preaching Meet* (Nashville: Abingdon, 1995); Lucy Atkinson Rose, *Sharing the Word: Preaching in the Roundtable Church* (Louisville: Westminster John Knox, 1997).

Chapter 2 • Frames for Approaching Contexts

1. John Lofland and Lyn H. Lofland, *Analyzing Social Settings: A Guide to Qualitative Observation and Analysis*, 3d ed. (Belmont, Calif.: Wadsworth, 1995), 3–5.

2. Wayne C. Booth, Gregory G. Colomb, and Joseph M. Williams, *The Craft of Research*, 2d ed. (Chicago: University of Chicago Press, 2003), 40–74.

3. Peter Reason and Hilary Bradbury, eds., *Handbook of Action Research: Participative Inquiry and Practice* (Thousand Oaks, Calif.: SAGE, 2001); William Foote Whyte, ed., *Participatory Action Research* (Newbury Park, Calif.: SAGE, 1991).

4. Max L. Stackhouse, "Contextualization, Contextuality, and Contextualism," in *One Faith, Many Cultures: Inculturation, Indigenization, and Contextualization*, ed. Ruy O. Costa, The Boston Theological Institute Annual, vol. 2 (Maryknoll, N.Y.: Orbis, 1988), 10.

5. Preaching therefore exemplifies the work typical to the field of practical theology, which "carefully examines faithful practices that happen especially in *local and nearby situations*." Kathleen A. Cahalan and James R. Nieman, "Mapping the Field of Practical Theology," in *For Life Abundant: Practical Theology, Theological Education, and Christian Ministry*, ed. Dorothy C. Bass and Craig Dykstra (Grand Rapids: Eerdmans, 2008), 62–85.

6. Rudolf Bultmann, "Is Exegesis without Presuppositions Possible?" in *Existence and Faith: Shorter Writings of Rudolf Bultmann*, trans. Schubert M. Ogden (New York: Meridian, 1960), 289.

7. Frames therefore have an external and internal quality. The former is emphasized in organizational studies when describing vantage points on a territory or cognitive lenses for finding our way around; see Lee G. Bolman and Terrence E. Deal, *Reframing Organizations: Artistry, Choice, and Leadership*, 3d ed. (San Francisco: Jossey-Bass, 2003), 12–13. The latter is emphasized in the ethnography when describing the shared knowledge of group participants (comprised of so-called cultural scenes) that defines some aspect of their common experience; see James P. Spradley and David W. McCurdy, *The Cultural Experience: Ethnography in a Complex Society* (Prospect Heights, Ill.: Waveland, 1972), 24–31.

8. In the typical ethnographic pattern of collecting, narrowing, and analyzing mentioned earlier in this chapter, this later iterative use of framing is part of the "narrowing" phase in which researchers take the amassed data and pose distinctive questions, categorize significant patterns, and highlight compelling features. For a detailed description of how this happens from a social science perspective, see: Lofland and Lofland, *Analyzing Social Settings*, 99–178; Michael H. Agar, *The Professional Stranger: An Informal Introduction to Ethnography*, 2d ed. (San Diego: Academic, 1996), 167–84.

9. James R. Nieman and Thomas G. Rogers, *Preaching to Every Pew: Cross-Cultural Strategies* (Minneapolis: Fortress Press, 2001), 23–27, 57–61, 114–17.

10. Ibid., 139–47.

11. Bolman and Deal, *Reframing Organizations*, 44–45, 115, 186–89, 242–43. For a different set of frames or lenses related to these but more attuned to congregations, see Nancy T. Ammerman, Jackson W. Carroll, Carl S. Dudley, and William McKinney, eds., *Studying*

Congregations: A New Handbook (Nashville: Abingdon, 1998). The approach advocated in congregational studies blends portions of the cultural category (frame as border) and organizational category (frame as structure) treated separately in the present chapter.

12. In this regard, it is important to note that entire organizational analysis of frames was developed in direct relation to larger questions of effective leadership. Bolman and Deal, *Reframing Organizations*, 301–434.

13. Robert J. Brym and John Lie, *Sociology: Your Compass for a New World*, 2d ed. (Belmont, Calif.: Wadsworth, 2005), 110–11.

14. Peter L. Berger and Richard John Neuhaus, *To Empower People: The Role of Mediating Structures in Public Policy* (Washington, D.C.: American Enterprise Institute for Public Policy Research, 1977), 2.

Chapter 3 • Tools for Exploring Contexts

1. Chief among these are the Web sites of the United States Census Bureau (http://www.census.gov) and the Association of Religion Data Archives (http://www.thearda.com). The Hartford Institute for Religion Research Web site provides links to many sorts of online information (http://hirr.hartsem.edu); all accessed February 28, 2008.

2. The many excellent and extensive guides to participant observation include Kathleen M. DeWalt and Billie R. DeWalt, *Participant Observation: A Guide for Fieldworkers* (Walnut Creek, Calif.: AltaMira, 2002); Danny L. Jorgensen, *Participant Observation: A Methodology for Human Studies* (Newbury Park, Calif.: SAGE, 1989); James P. Spradley, *Participant Observation* (Belmont, Calif.: Wadsworth, 1980).

3. Even with your particular focus for research, any event involves six broad features that suggest a more comprehensive view: (1) *Demography*—the social characteristics of the people involved; (2) *Location*—the site where activity occurs and how it relates to adjacent locales; (3) *History*—the past or traditions for this event and how people remember this; (4) *Organization*—the formal structures by which things happen, as well as informal or marginal roles; (5) *Activities*—the specific work that occurs, and at weekly, monthly, or annual patterns of time; and (6) *Means*—the resources in terms of finances, goods, and people, including what these enable or symbolize.

4. For ministers who have completed a basic unit of Clinical Pastoral Education, this is similar to writing a verbatim of a critical incident during chaplaincy. It is surprising how much of these events can be accurately remembered and how revealing the notes about them turn out to be.

5. Several kinds of interviews, including the semi-structured variety, are discussed in Robert Atkinson, *The Life Story Interview* (Thousand Oaks, Calif.: SAGE, 1998); David M. Fetterman, *Ethnography: Step by Step*, 2d ed. (Thousand Oaks, Calif.: SAGE, 1998), 37–52; James A. Holstein and Jaber F. Gubrium, *The Active Interview* (Thousand Oaks, Calif.: SAGE, 1995); and James P. Spradley, *The Ethnographic Interview* (New York: Holt, Rinehart, and Winston, 1979).

6. An example of a simple yet generative list of questions appears in James R. Nieman and Thomas G. Rogers, *Preaching to Every Pew: Cross-Cultural Strategies* (Minneapolis: Fortress Press, 2001), 19.

7. Most of the pertinent literature can be found in the area of material cultural studies: Colleen McDannell, *Material Christianity: Religion and Popular Culture in America* (New Haven: Yale University Press, 1995); David Morgan, *Visual Piety: A History and Theory of Popular Religious Images* (Berkeley: University of California Press, 1998); and Thomas G. Schlereth, ed., *Material Culture: A Research Guide* (Lawrence: University Press of Kansas, 1985).

8. Even with these questions, be cautious about several typical errors that introduce distortions. These include: (1) isolating the product from its typical setting, where it becomes an object unto itself; (2) over-attributing significance to the product, where it is made to say more about the context than it really can; (3) functionalist interpretations, where the aesthetic or symbolic dimensions are lost; (4) abstracted significance, where the concrete quality or use is minimized; (5) intentional fallacies, where the originator's purpose becomes the only valid explanation; (6) present-time errors, where the investigator's time period dominates the interpretation; and (7) progress-continuum errors, where biases about the past or present are implicitly justified in how the product is interpreted.

9. Recent resources on document analysis include: Ian Hodder, "The interpretation of documents and material culture," in *Collecting and Interpreting Qualitative Materials*, ed. Norman K. Denzin and Yvonna S. Lincoln (Thousand Oaks, Calif.: SAGE, 1998), 110–29; Gary McCulloch, *Documentary Research in Education, History and the Social Sciences* (New York: RoutledgeFalmer, 2004); Lindsay Prior, *Using Documents in Social Research* (Thousand Oaks, Calif.: SAGE, 2003); and David Silverman, *Interpreting Qualitative Data: Methods for Analyzing Talk, Text and Interaction*, 3d ed. (Thousand Oaks, Calif.: SAGE, 2006), esp. chap. 4, "Texts."

10. Despite our familiarity with texts and therefore our tendency to gravitate toward this tool, there are several potential limits that can preclude the effective use of documents. Some texts may simply be *unavailable* due to lack of production, limited survival, or poor condition. Otherwise available material may have *restricted access* due to gatekeepers or other barriers. Problems with language, clarity, codes, or lack of a frame of reference may present *interpretive* difficulties. Certain *ethical conditions* may mean that the use or reporting of some documents would produce harm. Finally and paradoxically, we may face *overly abundant* materials, so numerous or widely scattered as to be unfeasible for our use.

11. Of course, documents rarely fall neatly into these categories and are usually rather mixed and hybrid. For example, autobiographies are eyewitness documents (primary) yet often written long after the events (secondary). Scholarly texts use primary works (secondary) but reflect the concerns of their own period of composition (primary). Diaries (primary, of a life) are edited or translated when published (secondary, in the world). Letters (unsolicited) may have a masked or unacknowledged public agenda (solicited). Finally, archival materials (for a place) are public but usually originate quite privately (of a life).

12. An ethical question is often raised at this point. Is it right to study your congregation in this fashion, and to what extent should members know about it? The consensus today is that the kind of fieldwork described in this chapter should be "transparent," so that those you study realize they are contributing to your research. That said, you are not an anthropologist using these insights for outside publishing or professional aims. Instead, you were called to serve the place where you preach, which confers both the authority to understand it better for pastoral leadership and the rationale to engage it more deeply for your preaching. By all means, be open with the congregation that you are intentionally trying to learn about your mutual work for the sake of better ministry. Invite them to join in that process as they are willing and able, and assure your accountability to them by summarizing your insights when your contextual study concludes. Such transparency does not obligate you, however, to let others to look over your shoulder, manage how you proceed, or scrutinize your private reflections. As with many other pastoral acts (like confession or counseling), boundaries on all sides should be respected and involvement must be voluntary. Fortunately, because congregations are complex systems, non-participation by some need not obstruct your contextual study. There are many other avenues by which you can learn while respecting the dignity and concerns of various members.

Chapter 4 • Signs for Interpreting Contexts

1. Excellent basic resources on semiotics and its social implications include Daniel Chandler, *Semiotics: The Basics* (London: Routledge, 2002); Robert Hodge and Gunther Kress, *Social Semiotics* (Ithaca: Cornell University Press, 1988); Winfried Nöth, *Handbook of Semiotics* (Bloomington: Indiana University Press, 1990); and Theo van Leeuwen, *Introducing Social Semiotics* (London: Routledge, 2005).

2. St. Augustine, *On Christian Teaching*, trans. R. P. H. Green (New York: Oxford University Press, 1997), 30–100 [Books Two and Three].

3. For clarity, we refer to *all* such "packages" of signifier, signified, and signification as "signs," avoiding the arcane discussion that distinguishes signs from "symbols" or other specific terms in the vocabulary of semiotics. The most valuable of these distinctions can still be maintained by simply speaking of different kinds of signs, rather than resorting to alternative terminology.

4. Even so, this double gaze still happens within our ordinary experience. The further meaning of a sign is only seen through additional effort since this meaning, like the form of the sign itself, is thoroughly embedded in everyday existence. In a similar way, Edward Schillebeeckx noted how religious experience was inseparable from ordinary human experience. "Religious experiences display the same structure as our other human experiences: they are clearly related to human experiences of revelation, but express a dimension of depth in these human experiences. One has religious experiences in and with particular human experiences, though with the illumination and help of a particular religious tradition in which people stand and which is thus influential as an interpretative framework which provides meaning." Edward Schillebeeckx, *Church: The Human Story of God* (New York: Crossroad, 1990), 24.

3. These terms originate from two sources (although their use in this book differs in several specific ways): Charles S. Peirce, *Collected Papers*, ed. Charles Hartshorne and Paul Weiss, vol. 2, *Elements of Logic* (Cambridge: Belknap Press, 1931–1958), 247; and Erving Goffman, "Tie-Signs," in *Relations in Public: Microstudies of the Public Order* (New York: Basic Books, 1971), 188–237.

6. Mircea Eliade, *Images and Symbols: Studies in Religious Symbolism* (Princeton: Princeton University Press, 1991), 163–78.

7. Rudolf Bultmann, "Christmas," in *Existence and Faith: Shorter Writings of Rudolf Bultmann*, trans. Shubert M. Ogden (New York: Meridian, 1960), 278.

8. The phrase is from Thesis 21 of Luther's 1518 Heidelberg Disputation. Jaroslav Pelikan and Helmut T. Lehmann, eds., *Luther's Works*, vol. 31, *Career of the Reformer I*, ed. Harold J. Grimm (Philadelphia: Muhlenberg, 1957), 53. See also Gerhard O. Forde, *On Being a Theologian of the Cross: Reflections on Luther's Heidelberg Disputation, 1518* (Grand Rapids: Eerdmans, 1997), 81–90.

9. In a similar way in relation to preaching, Fred Craddock famously examined an adage by Søren Kierkegaard about the difficulty of speaking about Christian faith in a society that has heard it all before. Craddock noted that the problem largely rested with our tendency to be unduly direct, using the most blunt means for saying what we want to convey. The alternative he proposed was indirectness, looking for alternative routes in preaching and oblique avenues of disclosure. Fred B. Craddock, *Overhearing the Gospel: Preaching and Teaching the Faith to Persons Who Have Heard It All Before* (Nashville: Abingdon, 1978).

10. The Russian formalist Victor Shlovsky referred to this move as "defamiliarization," the idea that poetic language takes something commonplace and renders it unusual and wondrous again. Victor Shlovsky, "Art as Technique," in *Russian Formalist Criticism: Four Essays*, trans. Lee T. Lemon and Marion J. Reis (Lincoln: University of Nebraska Press, 1965), 3–24.

11. Peter L. Berger, "Theological Possibilities: Starting with Man," in *A Rumor of Angels: Modern Society and the Rediscovery of the Supernatural* (New York: Anchor, 1990), 55–85.

12. Nancy T. Ammerman, Jackson W. Carroll, Carl S. Dudley, and William McKinney, eds. *Studying Congregations: A New Handbook* (Nashville: Abingdon, 1998), 43–47, 209–10; Carl S. Dudley and Nancy T. Ammerman, *Congregations in Transition: A Guide for Analyzing, Assessing, and Adapting in Changing Communities* (San Francisco: Jossey-Bass, 2002), 59–70.

Chapter 5 • How Preaching Works with Context

1. Sidney Harris, *What's So Funny about Science? Cartoons by Sidney Harris from American Scientist* (Los Altos, Calif.: William Kaufman, Inc., 1977).

2. Edwin H. Friedman, *A Failure of Nerve: Leadership in the Age of the Quick Fix*, ed. Margaret M. Treadwell and Edward W. Beal (New York: Seabury, 2007), 83.

3. Justo L. González and Catherine G. González, *The Liberating Pulpit* (Nashville: Abingdon, 1994), 47–52.

4. Gerd Theissen, *The Sign Language of Faith: Opportunities for Preaching Today*, trans. John Bowden (London: SCM, 1995); Gail Ramshaw, *Treasures Old and New: Images in the Lectionary* (Minneapolis: Fortress Press, 2002).

5. Paul Janowiak, *The Holy Preaching: The Sacramentality of the Word in the Liturgical Assembly* (Collegeville, Minn.: Liturgical, 2000).

6. Paul Scott Wilson, *The Practice of Preaching*, rev. ed. (Nashville: Abingdon, 2007), 187–207.

7. James R. Nieman, "Preaching that Drives People from the Church," in *A Reader on Preaching: Making Connections*, ed. David Day, Jeff Astley, and Leslie J. Francis (Aldershot, UK: Ashgate, 2005), 247–54.

Representative Readings

Ammerman, Nancy T., Jackson W. Carroll, Carl S. Dudley, and William McKinney, eds. *Studying Congregations: A New Handbook*. Nashville: Abingdon, 1998. An accessible research guide for studying congregations that relies on an organizational framing of churches; somewhat spare on theological analysis.

Bolman, Lee G., and Terrence E. Deal. *Reframing Organizations: Artistry, Choice, and Leadership*. 3d ed. San Francisco: Jossey-Bass, 2003. A detailed treatment of many business examples using an organizational framing, yet still quite adaptable in reference to congregations.

Chandler, Daniel. *Semiotics: The Basics*. London: Routledge, 2002. A wide-ranging orientation to the entire discipline that studies signs and symbols; the initial chapters are more likely relevant for preachers.

Denzin, Norman K., and Yvonna S. Lincoln, eds. *Collecting and Interpreting Qualitative Materials*. Thousand Oaks, Calif.: SAGE, 1998. A good overview of the entire range of qualitative research but with a special section on artifact study and document analysis.

DeWalt, Kathleen M., and Billie R. DeWalt, *Participant Observation: A Guide for Fieldworkers*. Walnut Creek, Calif.: AltaMira, 2002. A current and comprehensive discussion of the manifold details of participant observation methods and challenges.

Hodge, Robert, and Gunther Kress. *Social Semiotics*. Ithaca: Cornell University Press, 1988. A lively and fascinating treatment of an important subfield in semiotics that attends far less to texts than to social situations and interactions.

Janowiak, Paul. *The Holy Preaching: The Sacramentality of the Word in the Liturgical Assembly*. Collegeville, Minn.: Liturgical, 2000. A theological reclaiming of the "sacramentality of preaching" that suggests how proclamation can engage both worship and Scripture in deeper ways.

Lofland, John, and Lyn H. Lofland. *Analyzing Social Settings: A Guide to Qualitative Observation and Analysis*. 3d ed. Belmont, Calif.: Wadsworth, 1995. A step-by-step overview of various ethnographic fieldwork procedures with special attention to participant observation and interviewing.

Nieman, James R., and Thomas G. Rogers. *Preaching to Every Pew: Cross-Cultural Strategies*. Minneapolis: Fortress Press, 2001. An interview-based study of effective cross-cultural preachers that demonstrates both an interview methodology and a cultural framing strategy.

Schreiter, Robert J., *Constructing Local Theologies*, Maryknoll, N.Y.: Orbis, 1985. A classic in contextual theology, explicating the many ways in which particular groups are thoroughly and often surprisingly theological.

Silverman, David, *Interpreting Qualitative Data: Methods for Analyzing Talk, Text and Interaction*. 3d ed. Thousand Oaks, Calif.: SAGE, 2006. A mixed-method approach to several qualitative tools but with special attention to the analysis of conversations and documents.

Spradley, James P. *The Ethnographic Interview*. New York: Holt, Rinehart, and Winston, 1979. An older yet still compelling discussion on interviewing methods and challenges that is attuned to qualitative rather than quantitative outcomes.

Theissen, Gerd. *The Sign Language of Faith: Opportunities for Preaching Today*. Trans. John Bowden. London: SCM, 1995. An expansive discussion of scripture from a semiotic perspective, suggesting the many biblical patterns and moves that contextual preachers can engage.

Tisdale, Leonora Tubbs. *Preaching as Local Theology and Folk Art*. Fortress Resources for Preaching. Minneapolis: Fortress Press, 1997. An intuitively driven approach to paying attention to the basic theologies at work in congregations and what preachers might do with them.